# The Creative Band & Orchestra

## By Julie Lyonn Lieberman

## The Creative Band and Orchestra
by Julie Lyonn Lieberman

Published by: Huiksi Music, Post Office Box 495, New York, NY 10024 U.S.A.

**Cover Design:** Michael Snow, SnowCreative.com
**Background Cover Art:** Four superimposed canvases by Si Lewen, http://www.silewen.com/
**Cover Art:** Eddy Cruz, Denisse Garcia, and Aliza Martinez
**Graphic Design:** Julie Lyonn Lieberman
**Editor:** Dawn Schloesser
**Copyeditor:** Joanna Dalin
**Photographs:** Carey Weiss
**Photo Shoot:** Courtesy of Marcia Rhoades and students from Pelham, New York, Middle and High School
**Single Line Drawings:** Sir Shadow, www.sirshadow.com
**Children's Illustrations:** Courtesy of Rachel Farmer and her 3rd grade students from Community Elementary School 11, Bronx, NY: Eddy Cruz, Jacqueline Torres, Joylyce Flowers, Erika Santiago, Aliza Martinez, Simone Sealey, Denisse Garcia, Carmen Milanes, Yukerlis Carrero, Jason Arroyo, Camille Diaz, Genessis Reyes, Jovanni Garcia, Andres Espinal, Anthony Garcia, Luis Hinojosa and Nia Thompson.

Copyright 2002 by Huiksi Music
First Printing
Printed in the United States of America
Includes Index.
1. Music  2. Improvisation  3. Ensemble  4. Band  5. Orchestra  6. Musicians

Visit **JulieLyonn.com** to see information on Ms. Lieberman's books, videos, and clinics.

### Acknowledgements and Dedication

Heartfelt thanks and acknowledgements to those individuals who have offered me so many life-changing experiences. A number of special mentors have helped facilitate my awareness of new approaches to creativity, music-making, and improvisation:

Dancer Micki Wesson of the Creative Arts Group Studio and cellist Gwendolyn Watson of the Connecticut College American Dance Festival in the sixties; Mike Delcig's Guerrilla Theater company at Rutgers University and Meyer Kupferman at Sarah Lawrence College in the seventies; David Darling and Paul Winter in our New England romp in the early eighties; and The Performance Workshop taught by vocal coach Ray Harrell and composer Ken Guilmartin in the eighties.

Additional thanks to Loren Moss and Michael Snow for their assistance on the layout; Rachel Farmer, for inspiring her students to create art for this book; Jan Farrar-Royce for her helpful feedback; and to the wonderful educators who enriched the contents of the book with descriptions of their creative approaches to working with groups, as well as the esteemed educators who endorsed this creative work.

**This book is dedicated to my mother, creative drama specialist Dr. Rosilyn Wilder, whose fertile imagination and ability to elicit wondrous elation out of groups of all ages has been a lifetime inspiration and model for me.**

# Foreword

We have a responsibility to our students.

This responsibility goes beyond teaching them what we think they should know based on our own personal aesthetics or background. The music world keeps changing, and the expertise we needed to develop to earn a living yesterday isn't what's required of the average musician or educator today. Our students need to be able to play within diverse styles, to read music well, and also, to create music through improvisation, composition, and arranging.

Today's educators must prepare our students with the skills they'll need to function well in their professional lives, whether they become professional musicians or music educators or not.

*The Creative Band and Orchestra* offers a perspective on teaching and making music that includes engendering spontaneity, exceptional group interaction, and focused listening, as well as an appreciation for, and understanding of, multi-cultural music — all through the art of improvisation.

The skills presented in this book can actually be useful to individuals in any walk of life. By the time many of us reach adulthood, we need to take special courses, such as those by Dale Carnegie, to build our self-image. Learning to improvise helps students develop greater self-confidence early in life. They learn to feel comfortable making decisions on the fly, or trying out different techniques until they discover what works best. When we encourage students to make their own music, to explore and define their own aesthetics, it's a form of validation. They are investigating how to express their individuality. Applying these capabilities within an ensemble, they are also learning how to bring that individuality into a group scenario in order to co-create and unify with others. In addition to becoming stronger musicians, they are learning to become stronger individuals, and also, stronger members of society.

Within *The Creative Band and Orchestra*, you'll find pages and pages of tools that will help you to help your students develop self-confidence, leadership skills, and enhanced creativity — both in the performance hall and outside of it.

**Justin DiCioccio**
**Chair of the Jazz Department at Manhattan School of Music**
**Conductor for the Grammy All-American High School Jazz Program**
**and The Henry Mancini Orchestra**

# Table of Contents

## ◈ GAMES AND TECHNIQUES ◈

## ◈ HANDOUTS ◈

## ◈ DIRECTORY OF ORGANIZATIONS ◈

## ◈ INDEX ◈

# Introduction

**L**et's dream big. Imagine that your orchestra or band can play jazz, blues, folk, pop, and Latin, as well as the classics. Members can improvise, compose, and write arrangements within all of the above styles. Electric sounds are included in tasteful ways, there is a cohesive and friendly environment, and no one is ever injured while playing. Most importantly, everyone looks forward to rehearsals and concerts.

It's time to update our teaching approaches to reflect the diverse musical tastes of our students, as well as our communities' audiences. It's time to liberate our imaginations and allow creativity to coexist with traditional allegiances. They aren't mutually exclusive.

*The Creative Band and Orchestra* offers a compendium of techniques, games, and relevant information and resources to help you create music for the new millennium. You can use the ideas in this book for bands, orchestras, choirs — ensembles of any size and style, from students to professionals.

Ideas aren't — and shouldn't be — owned by anyone. We are their caretakers and their vehicles, so feel free to modify the ones in this book to suit your needs.

**Julie Lyonn Lieberman**
**Julie@JulieLyonn.com**

# Orchestra on its EAR

# Bands & Orchestras Of The Future

## **B**AND

◆ TO BIND OR TIE TOGETHER

◆ TO ENCIRCLE

◆ TO BE TIGHT

◆ A BODY OF PERSONS BROUGHT TOGETHER BY A COMMON PURPOSE

◆ A RELATIVELY SELF-SUFFICIENT TRIBAL SUB-GROUP THAT IS MAINLY UNITED FOR SOCIAL OR ECONOMIC REASONS

## **O**RCHESTRA

◆ A CIRCULAR SPACE USED BY A GROUP

◆ A HARMONIOUS ORGANIZATION; THE INTEGRATION, OR COMBINATION OF DIVERSE ELEMENTS

**W**hat was renegade yesterday becomes the institution of tomorrow. Music is a living art. It breathes with, reflects, and counters the gestalt of any given cultures' beliefs and aesthetic values.

Ironically, every culture craves change as heartily as it relies on tradition. The desire for stimulation and the desire for foundation don't always coexist peacefully. Change can be difficult. Many issues and concerns can be activated, such as fear over the potential loss of tradition, discomfort in venturing out of the familiar, a commitment to values and standards that we fear will be compromised, and vague underlying myths that rarely prove true. For instance, some educators operate under the false belief that they have to give up everything they value in order to honor the musical tastes of their students. It *is* possible to maintain standards, advocate discipline, respect tradition, include the music of the world, and experiment!

### " Multi-Cultural Music "

For teachers who want to introduce multi-cultural music, I encourage them to listen, listen, listen! Listen to the music that is out there! Research via the Internet has become SO easy. A simple search, such as "Spanish folk songs," can elicit a number of websites where directors or teachers can find resources. Also, a search on a recordings website, such as Amazon or CDNow, is a great help. I make it a point to include music from other cultures in each concert. This includes selections of Celtic, African, Canadian, Mexican, Spanish, and Australian folk songs, among others.

Lori Elias
Willoughby-Eastlake City Schools, Ohio

# Honoring Tradition by Creating New Traditions

In recent years, we've seen creative individuals institute programs in their schools and states that include Mariachi bands, fiddling orchestras, competitions for original student compositions, and the incorporation of strings into jazz bands, to name a few.

When you show your students the options and honor their musical preferences, you are telling them that their opinion counts, and you are providing them with an experience that includes a level of enjoyment that will keep them asking for more. When you learn about your students' cultural backgrounds and include music in the repertoire that reflects the make-up of the group, you are promoting mutual respect and understanding.

If you want to try something that's never been done before, just remember that all that exists around us now is the culmination of centuries of imagination at play. We can honor the past by being the keepers of tradition, and honor the future by making our own contributions.

Embracing new approaches includes...

◆ incorporating games and techniques that feature improvisation, ear training, ensemble interaction, and playing healthy during warm-up and rehearsal;

◆ recognizing and honoring individuality through building repertoire that reflects our students' cultural heritage and musical tastes;

◆ changing the manner with which we interact by learning how to establish leadership without coupling it with authoritarian methods of communication; exploring styles from around the world;

◆ encouraging our students to compose their own works;

◆ changing our ideas about who sits where, when;

◆ experimenting with the use of technology.

# How To Get Started

Always start by asking your students what they listen to the most, and what interests them. If their response is one of silence, they might need suggestions to get them started. In fact, it may be more productive, depending upon the age and level of exposure of the group, to initiate this discussion after presenting them with possibilities.

Bring in a stack of CDs to introduce them to new styles. Try to expose them to new styles first through musicians who play their instruments. For instance, it's easier for a young clarinet player to identify with clarinetist Benny Goodman playing swing with a Big Band rather than pianist Count Basie, if he or she has never listened to jazz before. Playing examples from student groups can be inspiring, as well. Some of your examples can include groups like Barrage, or the Calgary Fiddlers, who've toured extensively and recorded. For additional inspiration, you can show the film, *Music of the Heart*, to demonstrate how obstacles can be overcome to create great music.

## " Mariachi "

Many of my students would not even be in music, would not be band-oriented, and might never have gone to college if it weren't for the Mariachi Program, but my Mariachi students *go into* college orchestra programs where they fit right in. Right now we have 100 violin players from fourth grade on up. When I first introduced Mariachi to my students, they were already falling out of line with their roots, especially the first generation from Mexico. They were listening to American music and their culture was disappearing. Mariachi music was being performed in commercial places, like restaurants, but not within the community.

Today, there are Mariachi programs all over the United States. The music is being performed by students from all different cultural backgrounds. In many cases, it is revitalizing music programs that had become outdated. It is our responsibility as the new generation to take Mariachi from the past and bring it into the future. We must uphold tradition and be conservative, but also bring to it our own flavor, because what we *do* today will become history.

The Mariachi program is a great alternative for a school who wants a violin program, but cannot afford a full orchestra. One can start with the more simple style of the Jarocho or Veracruzano style, which uses mostly first position and a lot of open strings, then proceed to the more conventional style of the Mariachi. Except for the Son Jaliciense style of playing, which uses a very aggressive style of bowing, the general Mariachi style is almost identical to the conventional orchestral way of playing. Mariachi repertoire even includes many of the classics.

Yamil Yunes
Director, Mariachi program
Roma, Texas

Projects can also inspire students to try new approaches. For instance, you can suggest hiring a famous pop artist to perform at your school, with the understanding that the students will accompany them on at least one piece. If the school doesn't have a budget for this, apply for a grant, or approach a local theater or concert hall. You can even approach the local sports team and arrange a performance of popular music by your students to open the game. Or how about finding an adult orchestra in your area and arranging an intergenerational concert that features styles that represent the community? The possibilities are endless.

## Technology

We live in a time when our students have grown up with at least one electronic gadget in their homes. Many of them are already using CD burners as well as the Internet, so it makes sense to take advantage of everything that's available. Using computers, software, and the Internet, we can generate original charts or accompaniments for practice exercises, and even communicate assignments through a central website. There are also some wonderful sites that we can use to assign fun ear training exercises (like www.good-ear.com). We can also incorporate the use of electronic instruments into our programs. When we use existing technology in concert with traditional approaches, we are staying current with our students' lifestyles and interests.

*I look at technology as being another tool for me to use with my teaching. I use many different types of technology, from CD players and recording equipment to computers and acoustic instrument MIDI interfaces. I am always using theory programs, simple sequencing programs, notation programs, and word processing programs with my students. I sometimes use sequencers to create music-minus-one types of accompaniments for my students to practice with and sometimes I might have the students do research about music history or composers by using the Internet. The uses are endless and the key for me is to make sure that I understand how the equipment or programs work before I introduce them to my students.*

*The main criteria I like to follow with technology is to find ways to use it without having to change the curriculum or teaching techniques. If using technology does not change the overall goal of a project or lesson, its use will be quite effective.*

Adam Davis
Maine South High School
Illinois

# Resource Material

In 2001, after spending years wondering how many closet composers had created new works for string players, I decided to create an interactive database on the Internet dedicated to alternative styles for strings. With the help of violinist and website designer Michael Snow, we created *StringsCentral.com* and began seeking contributors. Within the first few months after inception, we had fifty works for strings listed and a thousand visitors. We've continued to grow ever since.

Brand new advances require new tactics. If you are interested in incorporating alternative styles and approaches into your school's program, you can start by using the Internet, as well as state and national music organizations, to seek material. You may find what you're looking for, but if you don't, create it yourself by pressuring music publishers, raising money to hire composers or arrangers, organizing competitions, or writing/arranging material yourself or with your students. You might even consider creating a website where other educators can list what they've created.

## " Going Electric "

When I got my first electric violin no one had ever really seen one where I live. It didn't sound exactly like a violin but that was secondary, not just for the music I play, but especially in the educational arena. The electric violin allowed me to be a pied piper for exploring and sampling unfamiliar styles and helped encourage thinking out of the box about pre-existing technique and how to build upon it.

Similar to the guitar student who plays on both an acoustic and an electric at different times for different needs, the day is here for violinists to do the same. It's all about giving kids the permission to stretch the parameters of their overall musical experience. Electric violin doesn't alienate a students' classical roots but rather offers them the opportunity to integrate their techniques and musical background alongside the instrumentation and sound of their contemporaries. In other words, more and more violinists will be playing in their school orchestra as well as the neighborhood garage band too!

I also found that electric violins help facilitate recruiting students by initiating interest in non-players and also helps guard against burn-out by serving as an incentive to keep playing. "If I can learn (or continue) to play, then I can get an electric violin."

Cathy Morris
Electric Violinist, Educator
Indiana

# Listening with The Other Ear

When musicians come together to make music in a group, we assume they listen intently. But music-making uses so many mental and physical skills that the ears are often eclipsed.

We can view an object for its color, its texture, its size, its shape, its distance from us, and its dance with positive and negative space, or look directly at it and not consciously notice anything. The same is true for our ears. To transition from involuntary hearing to active listening takes intention and practice. We must activate new auditory perceptions through isolation exercises that involve learning how to activate the brain differently to create multi-level listening. When we do this, it's as if we've discovered a new way of hearing.

Think of the brain as a series of muscles. If one "muscle" is overused, it will become dominant, which can retard development in the other "muscles." The body/brain will keep funneling control into the stronger skill; it's a built-in default system.

By design — or by evolution — vision tends to dominate our other senses. The size of the visual cortex (the part of our brain that manages visual function) is considerably larger than the auditory cortex (the part of our brain that processes sound). Our culture bombards us with visual information through television, computers, and books, further increasing our reliance on sight. Then, as musicians, we keep "working out" the visual cortex when we stand at the music-stand "flexing our eyes" in order to make music. All of these factors conspire to dilute the development of our ears.

How do we strengthen our ears to improve our listening skills? Like any muscle you set out to strengthen, the ears must be singled out and exercised on their own. If you focus your ensemble members on listening first, allowing them to warm up the auditory muscle before they even look at the sheet music, you will help their brains to establish a hierarchy that's more appropriate to the act of making music. This is particularly important if they have just come from a series of classes, driving a car, or staring at a computer. The few minutes you spend re-tuning their brains will be well worth the time, because the whole session will be more productive. They will be listening rather than merely hearing.

Here's a familiar scenario in my studio: While I work mostly with musicians who are interested in learning how to improvise, I also work with classical players on ergonomic (playing healthy) techniques. When I teach these musicians, I sometimes single out a troublesome phrase in the music, and ask them to repeat it a few times with something new in mind (such as breathing, or releasing their thumb, or organizing how they move on their instrument differently). They will inevitably stare at the sheet music and, consequently, don't carry out the assignment very well.

If I swing the music-stand away from them, they often stumble, searching for the notes. Their first inclination is to use their eyes to organize the activity, by trying to look back at the sheet music. At this point, I force them to establish the phrase through ear training: I play it, they repeat it back. At first they might play awkwardly, but once their brain switches over from their eyes to their ears, there is a tangible moment when the fog lifts, and they truly hear the phrase — possibly for the very first time! At this point we can return to technical coaching on the phrase. They are now much more aware, in general, about body position, use of hands, intended sound, and so on. When we do turn back to the sheet music, we've established a different brain-to-ear-to-hand hierarchy, and their tone, as well as their musicianship, will show it for the rest of the lesson.

While this book is filled with exercises that help develop a listen-first hierarchy, here are some additional suggestions and exercises:

## Removing Visual Stimuli

Removing the musician's eyes from the process of making music can produce truly astonishing results. You can use a blindfold,

**VISUAL**

THE EYES TAKE A BITE OUT OF THE EARS!

THE AUDITORY CORTEX ACTUALLY TAKES LESS SPACE IN THE BRAIN THAN THE VISUAL CORTEX. BECAUSE WE LIVE IN A HIGHLY VISUAL SOCIETY (TELEVISION, COMPUTERS, BOOKS, CARS) WHERE WE "FLEX THE VISUAL MUSCLE" FAR MORE OFTEN THAN OUR OTHER SENSES, STUDIES HAVE REVEALED THAT OUR OTHER SENSES CAN SHUT DOWN AS MUCH AS 75% WHEN WE USE OUR EYES. WHAT DOES THIS MEAN TO THE READING MUSICIAN?

## AUDIATION

WHEN YOU AUDIATE, YOU ARE HEARING THE MUSIC INTERNALLY BEFORE YOU SOUND IT OUT THROUGH YOUR INSTRUMENT. BEETHOVEN USED THIS SKILL IN ORDER TO COMPOSE AFTER HE'D GONE DEAF. YOU CAN CULTIVATE THIS SKILL BY SINGING A MUSICAL PHRASE OUT LOUD AND THEN REPEATING THAT PHRASE SILENTLY, HEARING IT INSIDE. YOU SHOULD BE ABLE TO HEAR IT JUST AS DISTINCTLY. IF NOT, TRY A SHORTER PHRASE TO GET STARTED.

WHETHER WE ARE INTERPRETING A COMPOSED PIECE OF MUSIC OR IMPROVISING, WE SHOULD ALWAYS HEAR WHAT WE'RE ABOUT TO PLAY.

turn off the lights, play by candlelight, or ask everyone to close their eyes. Whichever method you use, you will hear a dramatic increase in the group's musicianship almost immediately. Members of the ensemble will listen more carefully and be more aware of how they use their bodies to produce sound.

Ask students to play the same passage of music, first staring at the sheet music, then at their instrument, and finally, off into the distance. Then turn off the lights or ask them to close their eyes and repeat the passage. You will never be disappointed by the results. The removal of visual stimuli helps create a focused tunnel through which the ears can hone in on not only the details, but also how those details come together to create the whole effect. Players may stumble at first to find their notes, but you can help them by singing or playing the phrase until they have it.

## Ear Training

You can use call and response exercises to isolate a rhythmic or melodic figure from the music as an ear training warm-up. For instance, choose a problematic passage and either sing, demonstrate (on your instrument), or ask a volunteer to play the first note of the phrase; the group will echo it back, then play the first two notes; the group echoes them back; and so on, until the group has repeated the whole phrase. If, at any point in this process, members of the group don't repeat the phrase perfectly, you can either simplify it again, or keep giving them that particular portion of the phrase until everyone is confident about the notes and/or rhythms.

This is a great exercise to help the entire ensemble learn one another's parts, particularly if the music is complex or if they aren't playing well together as a group.

## Listening Exercises

Audiation, the ability to hear the phrase or interval before we play it, is one of the more important listening skills we can help our students cultivate. Whether it's one by one or all at once, ask your students to choose a melody they know really well (like "Happy Birthday") and find it on their instrument. Then take a problematical phrase from your repertoire and play it for them slowly, asking them to try to hear the next note (or section of notes) before you actually play it. Encourage them to practice audiating at home.

You can also lead a partner game in which the "audiation specialist" (or whatever playful title you choose) has to anticipate what his/her partner is going to say and echo the partner's words back as quickly as he/she can. Kids do this all the time when trying to irritate their parents! When you practice anticipating another person's words and sentences, you have to exercise the same skills we need in music. This exercise will provide lots of fun while deepening your students' "other ear."

Just as we can change focus with our eyes, we can refocus our ears on sounds that are far away, or by degree, closer and closer. We can focus on the details of our own sound, or hear the totality of the group. We can also use images to facilitate changes in how we listen.

Ask the players to close their eyes and listen to the sounds around them. Start by bringing their attention to sounds that are outside of the room, and then gradually focus their ears on sounds that are closer and closer, until you ask them to listen to the rustling of clothing in the room, the buzz of fluorescent lights, or their own heartbeats.

Here's an example of another version of this exercise, requiring a mix of deep listening and imagination:

Tell the players:

*Close your eyes and listen to each sound as I describe it:*

*The timers on the traffic lights...the grass growing...trees swaying in the wind...people chewing their food in local restaurants...the sounds of the stars emitting light...*

*Now focus your ears on the sounds just inside this room...*

*Listen to the noise emitted by the lights in the room... the carpet decompressing...the floor boards lifting... your breath...your heartbeat...the blood moving through your veins...*

Add or substitute whatever images might be useful to your group.


## Recommended Reading

*The Listening Book* by Allaudin Mathieu
(Shambhala Press)

LEARNING BY EAR, RATHER THAN BY EYE, UTILIZES THE BRAIN IN A COMPLETELY DIFFERENT MANNER; ONE THAT IS MORE CONSISTENT WITH THE MENTAL HIERARCHY WE NEED TO BE TRULY GREAT MUSICIANS.

## Deep Listening

From childhood I have practiced listening.

As a musician, I am interested in the sensual nature of sound, its power of synchronization, coordination, release and change. Hearing represents the primary sense organ - hearing happens involuntarily.

Listening is a voluntary process that, through training and experience, produces culture. All cultures develop through ways of listening.

Deep Listening is listening in every possible way to everything possible to hear no matter what you are doing. Such intense listening includes the sounds of daily life, nature, and one's own thoughts, as well as musical sounds.

Deep Listening represents a heightened state of awareness and connects to all that there is. As a composer, I make my music through Deep Listening.

Deep Listening is active.

Listening is directing attention to what is heard, gathering meaning, interpreting, and deciding on action.

Pauline Oliveros
Distinguished Research Professor of Music
Rensselaer Polytechnic Institute Arts Department

# The Rehearsal Process

There are a number of givens when a group of musicians meet to rehearse: a great deal must be accomplished in a limited amount of time; time is eaten away by set-up; maintaining group focus can be challenging; and you must deal with uneven levels of playing ability, as well as varying states of preparation.

## Using Set-Up Time Constructively

Incorporating warmups when the students arrive can impact the nature of the rehearsal in a positive manner. For instance, using call and response, employing either melodic or rhythmic themes from the repertoire, will focus their ears, preparing them to listen more carefully once the rehearsal begins.

Stylistic or historic information could be presented. Volunteers from the previous session can be prepared to do this, or you can lead the presentation.

You can also teach the students an exercise routine to get them warmed up. Anyone who has unpacked first, instead of sitting around waiting or talking, can be stretching or swinging their arms, or practicing good posture. A small routine where players are required to do five reps of each of three or four warm-up exercises is beneficial to the group and gets students focused the moment they arrive. If you want to try this but don't have a clue as to what exercises to use, you can find exercises on Dr. Richard Norris's video, *Therapeutic Exercise for Musicians*, or my videos, *The Instrumentalist's/Vocalist's Guide To Fitness, Health and Musicianship* or *The Violin in Motion*.

I've watched string teachers tune their students' instruments one after another, trying to get it over with as quickly as possible. Instead, they could be using call and response to practice teaching the fifths, or ask the students to guess if the string is flat or sharp. Playing one game per practice session will only take a few minutes. The group will learn to listen actively, rather than be passive as the teacher does all the work. The students that can tune well could be helping those who can't. Sometimes we disempower others when we do too much and place doing it right, quickly, over teaching. The few extra minutes this approach would take will ultimately save time in the future.

# Sectional Work

During the rehearsal process, all leaders face the problem of how to rehearse one section of the group without boring the other sections. Players are usually instructed to be quiet, and aren't allowed to read or occupy their time other than by sitting still and waiting to be "reactivated." The idea is that they will learn something by listening to you work with another section. Not true. First, we have to teach them how to listen.

The best way to teach someone to focus the mind differently is through involvement, not passivity. Action instructs.

Create a game. Challenge students to listen for something specific within the other musicians' part. For instance, "How many times does the interval called a major third that we worked on in ear training show up in this passage? Is this a new theme, an old theme repeated, or a variation on the theme?" Or, "Listen to the other section rehearse their part and see if you can play the main theme from their part for me."

In addition to focusing on playing the music well, how about also addressing the elements that define the style? Pointing out the types of scale used, you can ask the whole group to play the scale central to a passage you intend to isolate with one or several sections. You can also point out interval preference within the melody, ornamentation, and rhythmic elements. This will help your students hear through new ears. If you don't have the training to outline the essential ingredients of the repertoire, CD liner notes, reviews, and historic or world music books can provide this resource material.

"Passive listening" means being told to listen, but having no idea what to focus on. Players are more likely to daydream or to start holding private conversations. "Active listening" is a state in which we become treasure hunters, searching for specific elements within the music.

# Communication Skills

As teachers, we often emulate the teaching style we experienced during our own studies. Unfortunately, the predominant teaching style of our predecessors tended towards a stern, admonishing, "You must suffer in order to improve" approach. However, when we speak with respect and purposefully seek and remark on the highest in each player, we help them to see themselves that way.

There is an unspoken presupposition built into certain styles of communication. For instance, if a teacher says, "That sounded terrible. Isn't anyone listening?" you can almost hear the subtext: "You don't care. You didn't try. You purposely didn't play that well."

But if a leader says, "Let's work together on improving that section," the subtext says, "Yes, we still have work to do on that part of the music, but I know you can do it."

I've met many young players who lost their enthusiasm for their instrument simply because they worked with teachers who pointed out problems in an extremely critical manner rather than supportively. It makes a big difference to say, "You played very well. Here's a little something you can do to improve that one spot…" versus following an attempt made by the student with, "You came in a half beat early on that section."

Most times, students already know whether or not they played well. If you aren't sure, you can ask them a question, such as, "Tell me everything that you liked about what you just played, and then identify the areas in which you had problems." Or, "Who in this section noticed a spot that didn't sound together? Where was it? Can you show everyone what it should sound like?"

> ## Orchestra
>
> I was thrilled when I got the good news that I'd been chosen to play in the first violin section of the regional orchestra. The acceptance meant even more to me when my local orchestra leader announced to my whole school that I'd been accepted into the most prestigious orchestra in the area. I felt very proud of myself.
>
> There were clues during the first few rehearsals that the orchestra might not live up to my expectations. The conductor gave each of us a chance to sit in the concertmaster's seat without any preparation, advice, or feedback. She laughed when the usual concertmaster made a nasty remark behind my back after I'd had my try. I felt hurt.
>
> We would rehearse for hours without a break, and when she rehearsed the cellos, she'd force us to listen, screaming, "Pay attention. This could pertain to you also." But we didn't have the cello part, and didn't have a clue as to what she wanted us to learn. We also had homework assignments for the next day at school, but we weren't allowed to read or do anything else when she rehearsed the other sections.
>
> No matter how much I practiced, she never acknowledged my hard work, only my mistakes — which I was already well aware of!
>
> I know that she had the best intentions to make everyone sound great, but a lot of the students felt dissatisfied and relieved when it was over. I won't miss that orchestra even though I had a chance to perform at Lincoln Center. I still have a bad taste from the experience.
>
> C. Healy
> Student violinist

# Teaching in Context

Before I became involved in performing alternative musical styles, I studied with over half a dozen fine private classical teachers. I don't remember any of them ever discussing the context within which each piece was composed, the identifying or significant features of the piece, signature structural elements, who composed it, or how it was received when first performed. I can't recall any of the music publishers including this information in any of the piles of sheet music I purchased during that time period. This information was designated to "music history," where it was taught in a very dry, unmemorable, and uninteresting manner.

When we rehearse music, that's the time to engage more than just our eyes and ears (see "Tapping Into New BrainStyles"). Let's make the music more relevant by thinking about more than printed notes.

"Notice how this composer (it doesn't hurt to repeat the composer's name each time you point something out) loves to jump an octave. Let's all practice playing octaves on our instruments. Everyone, play a 'C' note and then find it an octave higher. Now try it from a 'D' note."

Or: "This was written when he was 24 years old and had just received his first commission from the King. In those days, certain scales were considered too ethnic, and the King preferred music for dance, which put a strain on the composer, who wanted to be free to create the music he heard in his imagination. Can anyone here think of examples from your lives where money had to be placed before freedom?"

A date means nothing without context. "When this piece was written in 1844, there were no TVs, radios, sound systems, or telephones. How do you suppose everyone heard the piece?"

When we tell stories about the music, we have an opportunity to stimulate new perceptions and understandings that our students can apply to future music-making, as well as everyday life.

# Personalizing Your Seat

There are creative and fun ways that musicians can bring their individual touches to the rehearsal room. You can either coordinate this with the art department of your school or do it during a break. Wait for a special day, when you can see that your students just aren't in the mood to make music. Bad weather, the day before a holiday, or a day when local or world events have affected them are all good times to try this. Hand out magic markers, scissors, colorful paper, and any other art supplies you can find, and invite them to decorate their seat, the room, or both. If you decide to use rotational seating (discussed next), their artwork can move with them or be left for someone else to enjoy.

## Personalizing Dress

For years, we've encouraged our students to wear black or all the same color for performances. Black and uniform dress suggests teamwork, but also infers anonymity. As with all areas of life, sometimes tradition blinds us to the fact that we are free to create new choices.

Try encouraging students to dress individually. There can even be a theme for each concert. While uniforms may be necessary in certain contexts, there are many situations in which you can even invite them to decorate the stage and coordinate their dress to fit the theme of the decor.

## ADULTS AS MESSENGERS

ADULTS ARE THE FIRST MESSENGERS TO INFLUENCE OR SHAPE YOUNG PEOPLE'S IDEAS ABOUT THEMSELVES. STUDENTS ECHO, AND THEREFORE REINFORCE, THE MESSAGES THEY'VE LEARNED FROM YOU. YOU INFLUENCE WHAT THEY ARE ABLE TO ASK OF THEMSELVES, AND THEREFORE WHAT THEY ARE ABLE TO PRODUCE.

# Rotational Seating

The conductor of my high school orchestra was close friends with the parents of the concertmaster and his stand partner. He made no secret of this, or of the fact that those students were his personal favorites. The rest of us knew we would never be recognized, never sit in those first seats. In fact, we barely existed. The conductor looked at only those kids when he spoke, and even joked around with them before, during, and after rehearsal. The feeling of anonymity amongst the rest of the group promoted a sense of futility in our musical endeavors.

One day, the kids from the first two stands were absent because they were performing at an event in town. I was totally shocked when he invited us lowly players to move up. I ended up sitting at the first stand. I swelled with pride and played the best I'd ever played. I found that my attention was more focused. I even practiced more in the days that followed, until I returned to orchestra practice the next week to find that everything was back to normal. The magic was gone.

Isn't there enough competition in life? Why do we create — or even allow this — in our ensemble or classroom? What does this hierarchy communicate to each student psychologically, and is it really the message we want to send?

Years ago, a group of psychiatrists published a study on self-esteem. The researchers selected a class, and rearranged the seating after studying the performance of each student. They found that when students who habitually sat in the back of the room were moved to the front, both their classroom participation and their grades improved. The converse was also true.

Yes, we may very well need stronger leadership at the front of the ensemble during concerts but, as a student in the back of the room, I never heard our orchestra's "fearless leaders," because their backs were to me. I suspect, instead, that it's often the conductor who wants to be surrounded by the best in their inner circle. (After all, they never conduct from another spot in the room.)

During rehearsals, how about trying to mix things up a little bit? You can have fun with this, wearing a purple hat for random seating and a red hat for assigned seating. Figure out the fastest way to communicate how you want students to sit or move to another seat by making agreements the day before, or by presenting options when they arrive and taking a quick vote.

I like to ask students to play a game of tag when they first arrive. I tell them, "When you are tapped on the shoulder, play a long note and move to another position in the room. Tap the shoulder of someone else, and then take their position in the room." Then I get things started by tapping someone on the shoulder.

This game offers an off-handed way to get students comfortable with improvisation. After all, they are choosing what note they play, and for how long. Inadvertently, the whole seating plan gets changed around too!

You can even move around while conducting the pieces you've memorized. If you plan to tour with your group, this is a great way to train group members to be flexible about the spatial or acoustic challenges we inevitably experience when we perform in different concert halls.

When, and if, you put seating back into a traditional format, make sure your students know why each section traditionally sits or stands where they do, and why someone is selected to sit in the first stand. Most students don't have a clue. They don't realize that the instruments that are softer in volume are placed in front, and that the loudest are placed in the back. Students assume that the most skilled players are selected as leaders. But skilled in what? Technique? Musicianship? Leadership?

Playing skills can be one basis for selecting positions, but how about attitude? All too often, players who have been taught to be snobby by their teachers are put in roles of leadership. They set the tone for the entire group. Unfortunately, in my experience, it's usually the kids that come from privileged families that sit in front. Their parents can afford better instruments and lessons. This only intensifies the feelings of inadequacy the other kids may already be experiencing.

◆ Try a different seating plan within each section per rehearsal and concert;

◆ Try scrambling the entire group so that you have mixed instruments;

◆ Try switching stand partners on a regular basis;

◆ Stand in a different section of the group while conducting each rehearsal;

◆ Ask each section to take a vote on seating for the performance (by secret ballot) or select someone different to make up the seating plan for each concert;

◆ Invite different players to the podium to watch and listen to the group each rehearsal.

## Rotational Seating

When you compete for chairs, you end up with more losers than winners. You only have one or two kids, who got first or second chair, that are satisfied.

Just as frequently as it motivates the kids who 'lost' in some way or another to keep practicing, it makes them want to quit.

Rotational seating creates a friendlier environment. It gives orchestra members an opportunity to get along with each other, to get to know more members of the orchestra. It's non-competitive, since there's no focusing on who plays best. Rather, you're focusing on how good we can be as a group. It's a greater team-building philosophy. The students focus on how good the section sounds.

I really believe that rotational seating helps build depth. It builds more leaders, rather than just a small group of leaders. When the players rotate, a weak player, for example, is right under the nose of the conductor; they can't just hide out and sit in the back. There's no point in having somebody who feels like they're not a full time contributor. I really believe rotational seating is one of the things that's helped propel my program to be one of the top programs.

Jonathan Lane
Orchestra Director
Shawnee Mission East High School
Kansas City, Kansas

# Next Steps

When you rehearse using traditional seating, everyone's head tends to be buried in the music. The musicians don't listen to the other players' parts. Moving around the room helps them to hear the whole of the piece. Sitting in mixed sections means they have to fight harder to hold onto their own line, too.

To encourage familiarity with all of the parts, you can:

❖ Ask a section to clap the rhythms of a particularly problematic phrase of music and use call and response to involve the whole group, asking students to echo the section's part back;

❖ Repeat this exercise using either the students' voices, or their instruments, now adding the melodic line back into the problematic phrase;

❖ Switch parts for five or ten minutes, if possible. There are computer programs that will allow you to scan the music in and transpose it or change the clef, which can make this exercise easy to execute. But even if you allow the students to play the music in the wrong key, they will become more aware of how that part interfaces with their part. If you have an advanced group, why not ask the students to transpose the music themselves as a homework assignment? Some orchestra leaders are supplying all of their player's parts (in all three clefs) to everyone in the orchestra so that "sectional" work is always worked on by the entire ensemble!

# PURPOSE

Allowing students to sit in varying constellations enables us to foster deeper listening, and to cultivate equal leadership skills within the group, while creating a more cohesive ensemble.

Through the techniques outlined above, we can teach musicians to appreciate one another's roles within the group, create better ensemble interaction, stimulate feelings of self-value, and understand and play the music even better. After all, what can music possibly offer that's any different from other classes if we maintain the same tactics as class tests, tracking systems, SAT grades, report cards, and the like?

# INHERENT CHALLENGES

1) Time. These techniques are time-consuming for the teacher as well as the class. You will need to experiment with the techniques outlined above to figure out what will work smoothly and efficiently. Also, players that have been sliding by on the work of others may resent being put on the spot or having more asked of them. This is ultimately good for them, though. As they learn to rise to the meet the challenge and realize they can do it, they will automatically ask more of themselves in the future.

2) Attention span. It's best to try the techniques outlined above on more familiar music or small sections of pieces. Developing new listening skills can require capabilities that may not be readily available if someone is looking at music for the first time, or trying to play music that is particularly challenging to them.

# Innovative Scores

The music we herald as classic today challenged its listeners' ears and minds when it was first conceived. Any change does! And, whether we like it or not, everything is always changing. All of us have read about the growing pains many composers endured while creating works that were sneered at, criticized by the press, and even censored by kings. The term "way ahead of its time" is a familiar one when we study music history.

Over the years, as ears and minds caught up with these new sounds, the best of the best endured, and we still perform these works again and again all over the world. How many experimental pieces paid the toll to send each "classic" out into the future? Like Picasso's sketches for *The Guernica*, doesn't each composer or group of composers have to evolve their work to create one or two gems?

Music publishing is a big industry, and it relies on your budget and programs to exist. While it provides us with imaginative and ready-made scores, we tend to feel dependent upon the compositions that someone else has deemed worthy of performance. We forget that we could help develop the compositional skills of the musicians within the group. It's possible to create a balance between playing music written by dead — or living, for that matter — professional composers, and music written by our students and colleagues.

By composing their own pieces, members of your ensemble will be:

◆ practicing thinking and listening structurally;

◆ heightening their awareness of the essential ingredients of music, such as creating a beginning, middle, and end; building conflict into resolution; or introducing harmonic surprise;

◆ raising their self esteem by learning how to create something of their own;

◆ listening, compositionally speaking, for what could be;

◆ honoring the diverse musical tastes within the ensembles.

# Creating Interchangeable Parts

If flutists, let's say, play only lead melodies their whole lives, how can they possibly learn to appreciate the role that the bass line instruments play? Or even learn to listen to how the parts come together to create the whole? Most players listen too much to their own part. Why not compose parts that work no matter which instrument plays them so that everyone becomes familiar with one another's parts, as well as the role that those parts play in supporting the whole? A discussion afterwards can help clarify the role that each instrument traditionally plays in an ensemble.

With the use of computer software programs like Finale, we have the ability to scan a score into the computer and transpose it or change its clef. There are a number of grants available to teachers for software training as well as equipment purchases. Discuss this with your principal or department chairperson.

It's also useful to ask the students to transpose a part from another section to suit their instrument. But even if they play it in the wrong key, they'll still hear the melodic and rhythmic elements meant for a different section of the band or orchestra.

# Defining Style

When listening to music from different parts of the world, players gain an enormous amount from learning how to listen for details within the music, discussing what they hear, and answering questions like: "What makes this style unique?" or, "What helps define its musical personality?" This is because the instruments, scales, ornamentation, and aesthetics are so different from Western classical, folk, pop, or jazz. They are less likely to take unfamiliar sounds for granted.

To help facilitate students' listening skills as a prelude to writing their own pieces, you can steer their ears towards specific elements within the music, such as:

1) meter, and characteristics attributed to rhythmic phrasing;

>    Once identified, ask the group to clap some of the rhythmic phrases from the piece, and clap the time signature if it's unusual (for instance, odd meter).

2) key or tonal center(s) and type of scale used;

>    Let them use their instruments to try to figure out the scale(s) used in each piece; after identifying the scale, ask the group to play it.

3) ornamentation;

>    Point out embellishments unique to the style and practice playing them.

I use interchangeable parts in pieces that are part of one of my books. Each piece in the book has three string parts (A, B, and C) and an optional piano part. The three parts can be played just by themselves, or with a piano accompaniment or with the accompanying CD. They appear in each clef in each book so that they are interchangeable.

In a classic, traditional symphony, the cellos have nothing to do while the conductor practices the first violin part. Even without having the cellos play Line A in performance, it can still be very helpful in rehearsal. In a school setting, sometimes you will have very strong players in sections that may not have a whole lot to do in a traditional arrangement. So you can put a cello on Line A, and put the rest of the cellos on Line C.

The other helpful result of this arrangement is the fact that you can practice one part at a time. The kids can all practice line A, which gives the cellos something to do when you're practicing line A.

Martin Norgaard
Belmont University, Nashville
Author, Jazz Fiddle Wizard

## Creating Original Scores

When I was a kid, we played a game called "In My Grandma's Trunk There Was a...." It was a fun way to exercise memory. The first person says "In My Grandma's Trunk There was a..." (and they fill in the blank with any item they want). The next person repeats the opening phrase, including the item, and adds an item. Each person lists all the items recited before them, and adds one. It obviously gets more and more difficult to track over time as the list gets longer.

Seat the group in a circle. You might want to use the game described above to get group members warmed up. It evokes a lot of laughter and playfulness. Then translate the game into music. Ask someone to play a musical phrase, and then ask the next player to add onto it, and the next, and the next, and so on. Depending on what the group comes up with, you may want to make comments to point out important musical devices like theme and repetition, conflict and resolution, dynamics, and continuity. Then try it again. If a theme emerges that the group likes, this could become the basis of a homework assignment: Use this theme as the foundation for a whole piece of music.

Providing limitations can help structure how students proceed at home. For instance, you can ask them to write a specific number of measures based on the chosen theme, and then perform their composition for the class. You may even find it possible to create a longer group piece by patch-working their compositions together into one larger one.

# Culture or Style-Based Compositions

Creating original compositions within the ensemble can give group members an opportunity to share information about their ancestry. They can even bring in examples of music from their cultural backgrounds. I did this with my "Musicianship Through World Music" class at Juilliard. The information shared was surprising to everyone in the class. Even though the students were labeled "Latino" and "African American," we found that there wasn't a single student in the class who had the same genetic mixture or point of origin. It was extremely enriching to listen to the music of each family's heritage. I can even say that the students sat up a little straighter and looked upon one another differently after that!

If you don't want to be that personal with the group, you can also consider providing your ensemble with a list of styles, which could include:

| | | |
|---|---|---|
| - classical | - Flamenco | - Latin |
| - rock | - Celtic (Irish or Scottish) | - Asian |
| - blues | - Scandinavian | - African |
| - jazz | - Cajun | - Native American |
| - Calypso | - old-time | - Mexican |
| - Gypsy | - bluegrass | - Canadian |

Once the group has agreed on a specific style, create an accompaniment that embodies that style. You can do this by using the program "Band in a Box" by PG Music or find a CD with a piece of music on it in that style (Ellipsis Arts has an amazing world music catalog), and as a group, study the elements that help define the style, using them as a basis for creating a composition that's true to the genre.

Place limitations on the length, tempo, and any other elements to help get students started and keep them focused on specific variables. Using a Music Minus One accompaniment can help steer their ears in the right direction. There are blues, swing, and jazz accompaniments available from *Aebersold's Jazz Aides* (www.jazzbooks.com).

*Homespun Tapes* (www.homespuntapes.com) provides Celtic and bluegrass practice tapes. Sometimes finding sheet music for the chosen style helps the group analyze the ingredients of the style so that they can create something new. You can use the Internet to locate music.

If you make a group project out of it rather than a homework assignment for each individual, you can ask one person to design a melodic idea, another to make up a variation on the melody, a third to write the bass part or percussion part, etc., so that each individual brings some area of expertise to the project. Students can learn about how the copyright process works, and you can ultimately use a computer software program such as Finale, a laser-printer, and glossy paper to make the final piece look professional.

# Flexi-scores

A flexi-score consists of a visual or verbal guideline that allows for improvisation and individuality within the group. The flexi-score doesn't require a particular level of proficiency because players can modify it to their level and even their musical tastes; it will also accommodate varying degrees of improvisation. There are different types of flexi-scores you can use, such as:

## 1) Soundstories

As we discuss on page 66, a soundstory is a narrated musical performance based on an actual story. The players describe and enhance the plot through improvised textures, melodies, and rhythmic motifs.

## 2) Interchangeable Parts

The group can develop short melodic and rhythmic themes, notate them, and then create an improvised ensemble piece during which each ensemble member can choose the order in which they perform these themes.

## 3) Pictorial Scores

In the sixties, experimentation within the New Music community produced a number of pictorial scores that required interpretation by its performers. This provides a beautiful balance between relying on commands through the eyes — something the reading musician feels more comfortable with — and improvisation. You and/or your ensemble can break out of the linear mold and create an original score. Each time you perform it, the music will be different. Here's an example:

Play the motifs on this page as many times as you want in any order.
Interpret any symbol into sound, and listen, listen, listen...

**Pulse Pulse Pause Pause Pulse Pause Pulse**

**Try to sound like an ocean wave.**
**Try to sound like an alien landing on an ocean wave.**
**Try to sound like a clock ticking backwards.**
**Try to sound like silence while making sound.**

Stephanie is a first-year violin student. She is adorable and VERY nice, but small and frail and not well coordinated. She doesn't catch on to reading or concepts as quickly as most of the kids in her class and is often withdrawn and appears close to tears. One day she came in all excited (so excited that she dropped her music off the stand and then dropped her violin on the floor — no damage, fortunately!) because she wanted to play the piece that she'd just written for her mother's birthday.

She defined the parameters of her piece (like we do in our improvisation exercises). It had to be only on the D string (the string she knows all the notes on) and she could only use quarter notes, 8th notes and rests. Stephanie has a hard time controlling her bow for notes longer than a quarter note.

She was able to present these parameters as POSITIVES in her piece. She played her piece. She got the meter right. She got the notes in tune. Her musical lines made sense and she had a pretty good question-answer format to her tune. Everyone applauded wildly — and honestly! And then the kids all asked to learn Stephanie's tune! Stephanie blushed deeply. She stuttered with the pressure but she also glowed. We put aside most of the rest of our lesson while everyone learned Stephanie's tune by Stephanie playing a few notes at a time for us!

As the kids left my class I said something personal to each of them. Stephanie clearly hung back to be the last out. "Can I give you a hug?" I asked. She smiled. She had tears in her eyes!

"What you did today was so special ," I began. I tried to elaborate but Stephanie knew better than I did everything she had accomplished today. "This is a day, Mrs. Royce, I will NEVER forget!"

"This is the first of what could be MANY days like this for you, Stephanie," I said. "Maybe you'll be inspired to write another tune for us someday soon?"

She BEAMED and literally SKIPPED out the door. And I have tears in my eyes AGAIN as I recollect this story.

Janet Farrar -Royce
Orchestra Director
String Teacher
Cheshire, CT

# Tapping Into New BrainStyles

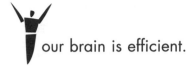 our brain is efficient.

Once the brain learns a new activity, its preferred style of action is to economize on energy and send the same instructions the same way. Building new methods to process information takes energy, and I sometimes think that the avoidance and resistance many of us experience emotionally when exposed to new areas of work or ways of thinking may come from our brain's natural defense system against exertion.

For all we know, when we, or our students, want to stomp our feet and say, "I don't want to, I don't want to," or, "I feel like my brain just glazed over," this may very well be the result of a released chemistry. Much the way the squid squirts blue ink around itself for protection, the brain may be issuing an emotional smoke-screen to prevent change!

## Gesture Versus Detail

When we learn something for the very first time, our brain processes the general shape of it first. The transition from gesture to detailed control is a willful process. For the most part, we don't focus on detail automatically. We have to prompt our mind to hone in on detail. It's an intentional and learned process. Whether it's the visual artist's transition from stick drawings to sketches that are three-dimensional, or the musician's transition from good tone and good intonation to subtle coloration of the notes and phrases, the brain is actually building new facets of its web, connecting the cells of the honeycomb together into a more powerfully productive configuration. This takes time, and requires willful, detail-specific repetition.

A devoted mentor can facilitate this process. Devotion is required because it takes commitment, persistence, and tons of patience to inspire another individual to change, learn, or grow. We must resist the temptation to take the process personally: "This student must be ignoring my advice;" or to jump to false conclusions: "He/she must be lazy or stupid, or lacking talent." The mentor must show the student or group what to focus on, and teach them how to organize themselves mentally in order to gain mastery.

# The Primary Learning Centers

## Imagistic Memory

Imaging is the ability, with eyes open or closed, to practice a musical phrase or an entire piece of music in detail mentally. We are actually using our right hemisphere to create a "map in motion," which will prepare the mind-to-body hook-up so that the command center emanates from the mind, not the hands!

When you image, you are experiencing the act of playing as if you were actually playing your instrument, but without moving your body. This frees you to focus on breathing and relaxing the body, while playing the music mentally. Mental practice protects muscles from overuse, can be done anywhere (not just in the practice room), and is our most dependable memory center.

## Auditory Memory

The driving force behind music, auditory memory is the ability to hear the entire piece in your inner ear without referring to your instrument or sheet music. It's surprising how many musicians, when asked to hum or whistle the piece of music they're working on, have difficulty hearing the piece in their inner ear!

---

## Analytical Memory

This approach utilizes left-brain thinking to examine the internal structures and relationships within a piece of music. You can point out simple details, such as the key and time signature, how the melody flows in relation to the tonal center, intervalic relationships within problematical phrases, or any other structural relationships that might simplify the learning process. For example, it's far easier to learn a phrase of music by realizing that it's an upside-down arpeggio, or a scale-like run starting on the third of the key and flowing down to the fifth, than by trying to memorize each note for its own sake.

## Muscle Memory

Muscle memory utilizes the body's natural ability to learn sequences of motion. It's developed through consistent (and often, unfortunately, mindless) repetition. Eventually, the muscles are able to perform a series of moves with little or no conscious direction from the mind other than whatever is required to get started. Commonly used by musicians, but often not backed up solidly enough with other skills, muscle memory doesn't hold up well under performance conditions when the chemistry of nervousness floods the body.

A DISCRETE SENSORY RECORD OF A PARTICULAR GESTURE OR SERIES OF GESTURES IS CALLED A SENSORY ENGRAM.

Engrams encode not only the things I do repeatedly, they also encode the manner in which I do them, my style of doing. And even further, the things that I do the most often, and the manner in which I do them, begin to influence the style with which I do everything else.

Deane Juhan
Author, Job's Body

# From Competence to Performance

After a number of in-depth studies, the scientific community has concluded that it takes three hours of repetitive activity for the motor cortex (the part of the brain that communicates with muscle) to build a new sensory engram. According to the study, if the individual attempts to learn several brand new skills simultaneously, the learning process will be diluted, and take additional time.

I like to think of these engrams as bar-codes. They lock in every detail of information we've given ourselves with regard to the chosen activity. For instance, if you drill a passage of music for technical mastery while holding your breath, eventually, you will be able to perform that passage as technically intended, but you'll be likely to automatically hold your breath each time you play it. The nervous system says "yes" to whatever we ask of it, the muscles say "yes," and the motor cortex records it all. It can't discern between useful and dysfunctional information. It just says "yes."

The old teaching model that consists of "show and tell," where the teacher tells the student what to work on and the student comes back and shows the teacher what they've done, isn't as effective as rolling up your sleeves and getting down to it right then and there. It shouldn't just be about mastery; the teacher/student relationship should encompass teaching new ways to learn. The teacher not only passes information vital to the craft on to the student, but also teaches the student how to learn.

So, is it enough to just repeat a phrase over and over mindlessly? No.

The most effective route to learning is to make sure that the information has been recorded in each of our primary learning centers, and that the quality of approach has been included in the work process. This encompasses pursuing quality of sound simultaneous to quality of experience: breathing, lengthening the muscles rather than contracting or constricting them, and proper posture.

# Primary Modes of Communication

Everyone learns differently. For whatever magically mysterious reasons, we all have mental strengths and weaknesses, as well as different languages through which we perceive new information with the greatest clarity. If an extremely verbally-oriented teacher explains something with poetically profound language, sits back with pride, and watches their kinesthetically-oriented student (someone who learns better through touch and spatial awareness of his or her body) stare back at them dumbstruck, that teacher may think that this student is either stupid or not listening. Not true! They didn't hear you because they speak another language.

I teach the same musical activity through as many languages as I possibly can, for several reasons. First, I want to make sure my students get it! Secondly, each time I repeat the same instructions in a different way, I help them strengthen comprehension through varying languages. It would be like saying hello in English, Spanish, French, and German every day. Eventually, they'll recognize and remember the meaning each and every way.

For instance, let's say that you are working with a player on using the right arm in a certain position. You can first:

◆ **demonstrate:** this requires visual recognition and the ability to convert a visual image into a sensory experience;

◆ **explain it:** this requires the ability to process language into body moves;

◆ **use touch** to help them find the shape: this requires kinesthetic (feeling awareness) recognition;

◆ **use a kinesthetic aide:** this approach bypasses the conscious mind and fixes the muscles into a position until that position is recorded by the motor cortex (you can use an ace bandage, a sock with a ruler in it, a pipe-cleaner, or whatever else you can invent to help hold the students in the position you are trying to teach);

◆ **use an image** to describe the position: this requires a strong right-brain orientation;

◆ **use engineering lingo:** this is best for the mathematically adept (such as "place your elbow at a right angle").

Once students can successfully process the instructions by translating them into the correct physical position or style of motion, practice coming in and out of that position with them. This will help them to repeat the shape at will whenever they want. Ideally, if they've assimilated the information thoroughly, you can now layer in more complicated information regarding other parts of their hand or issues focused on musicianship, without their form falling apart.

Applying these concepts to musicianship, rather than technique, you can select a problematical passage and:

❖ isolate and sing, tap, or play (on a single note) the rhythms in the phrase;

❖ play the melodic line as quarter notes to isolate pitch-to-pitch motion;

❖ sing the melodic line two notes by two notes, for ear training and interval identification;

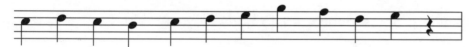

etc.

❖ put the instruments aside and mime playing the phrase with one hand at a time and then both together;

❖ name the notes while singing the phrase;

❖ name the fingerings while singing the phrase;

❖ put the rhythm and melody together, playing the phrase using an image to help define the musical feel.

# APPROACHES

## TO

# IMPROVISATION

# Why Teach Creativity?

Humans desire and need to create beauty. Our species is distinguished by its ability to create something from nothing simply for the pleasure of seeing it exist. This is a gift.

However, the Western European classical approach to teaching instrumental and vocal music — the one used until this century — often fails to make use of this great gift.

Instead of teaching them to create something from nothing, we're merely instructing our students how to replicate the art of those who have come before them.

This is akin to giving a person a car without the keys. An entire kingdom sits in wait, but you can't access it without something that exists outside yourself — that is, preprinted or memorized sheet music. Doesn't it strike you as odd that we can spend many years teaching an art that is totally inaccessible to our students unless they are staring at dots on a page, playing someone else's musical creations? As exquisite as the classics are, let's also teach our students how to make music spontaneously, without turning to memory or visual stimulation.

I have heard many players in workshop, learning to play by ear or improvise for the first time, comment that they have no idea what they're doing. Ironically, classical music tends to supply us with a false feeling of control, because we feel grounded by our eyes. The security we think we have when reading music is an illusion, though, because we're constantly afraid of making mistakes! Often, the best improvisations come from a clear mind and pure listening. You're not supposed to know what you're going to do next, or it wouldn't be an improvisation! Improvisers learn to fall in love with the uncertainty that leads to the thrill of discovery. They find pleasure in dancing on the edge of a cliff to freedom.

"Creativity"

Children, and especially middle school aged children, really need to express themselves — their own thoughts, feelings and opinions.

Improvisation gives them that outlet. As long as no one tells them that what they're doing is wrong, they can feel very good about what they create. Keeping it simple, by starting with one note in rhythm patterns, sets up a safe environment in which they feel free to, and excited to, create.

Barbara Carlsen
String Educator and
Conductor
Hastings, NY

It's so important to provide our students with the opportunity to experience music-making free of the fear of making mistakes, of not being good enough, or of making sounds outside of our conventional, cultural definition of aesthetics. Aside from the rich emotional benefits, we are also providing them with a chance to experience making music without the muscular tension associated with the effort to "play correctly."

While working as a consultant to National Young Audiences in the mid-eighties, I was sent to a school in the Midwest to help initiate a "build your own instrument" project. The principal took us on a tour of the school, proudly pointing out the amazing artwork on the school walls. At first I was fooled. I was impressed by the prolific exhibits in every hallway. Then, as if waking up from a dream, I realized with horror that only the colors were different. Every line drawing was identical: the classic farm couple standing in front of a barn. The art teacher had successfully taught the children how to draw correctly. In contrast, the children who made the artwork for this book used their imaginations to create one-of-a-kind drawings that reflect their unique perspectives. Their art teacher encouraged them to think, see, and express their individuality. While it's true that without technique, we have no tools with which we can make music, we tend to approach training young people as if creativity can't be expressed without technique.

The wonder of it is that we are all walking instruments. We each have a voice with which we can explore music in new ways. If anything, offering music as an "agenda-less" playful state of exploration will actually inspire young players to further their technical abilities.

# CREATIVE ORIENTATION

WHEN WE ORIENT OURSELVES CREATIVELY, WE SEE THAT WE CAN REINVENT OUR LIVES AND OUR SKILLS AT ANY MOMENT, AND WE CAN PASS THAT ABILITY ON TO OUR STUDENTS.

THE CREATION OF YOUR OWN UNIQUE SOUND ON YOUR INSTRUMENT IS SURPRISING. AT FIRST, LIKE A RUSTY FAUCET THAT HASN'T BEEN USED FOR A LONG TIME, YOU'LL SPIT OUT QUOTES FROM EVERYTHING YOU'VE EVER LEARNED. THEN, GRADUALLY, YOU WILL FIND YOURSELF LISTENING AS IF WITH NEW EARS; YOUR BRAIN WILL TILT SLIGHTLY TO PROVIDE AN INCREDIBLY REWARDING INTERCONNECTION BETWEEN YOUR EMOTIONS, YOUR PSYCHE, YOUR TECHNIQUE, AND YOUR WILL.

# From Fear To Fun:
## Teaching What You Don't Know

**M**any teachers say, "My students want to play different styles and learn how to improvise, but I feel phony teaching alternative styles and improvisation because I've only studied classical repertoire."

Don't let this stop you! Almost everything you introduce to your students will be brand new to them. You will be drawing from a lifetime of musical knowledge. The only thing that will be different is that you will apply that expertise in a new way. And if you do have students who are ahead of you, encourage them to teach what they know!

The fresh energy you bring into the classroom and rehearsal hall will engage and invigorate your players. When we do too much of the same thing too many times, we tend to fall asleep. It's comfortable, it's safe, but we aren't fully involved.

As you experiment with the games and techniques offered in this chapter, keep a few pointers in mind:

1) Every group is different — even if they're the same age. If an exercise isn't working, modify or simplify it to suit the group's capabilities, or move on to a another exercise. There's always something that catches each group. Once you find out what that "something" is, you can build from there.

2) When students express discomfort, you can help them move through their fear by: creating a duet with them, coaching them, trying call and response, or limiting them to a one-note improvisation within the game. If you truly see terror on their faces, it can be helpful to pass them by, and let them observe how other, more confident students participate. As they absorb the activity, they will naturally become involved and want to try it out.

> **"Improv"**
>
> Using improvisational tunes and exercises in my string classes has helped my students develop more accurate intonation and listening skills. It has given them more confidence in expressing themselves on their instrument and helped them to view their instrument more as their own musical voice. It has helped them to feel like music MAKERS, not just music players.
>
> Janet Farrar-Royce
> Orchestra Director
> String Teacher
> Cheshire, CT

Sometimes I create a spoken/sung duet with a reticent student. I take whatever they've said, like "No, I can't," or "I don't want to," and make a song or chant out of it. I invite the whole group to join in, conducting entrances and exits, dynamics, and so on. It's great fun, we get it out in the open and have a laugh, and from that point on, if anyone resists, I say "We've already sung that song. Let's move on."

Make it fun, show your willingness to participate, offer respect for the emotional component of the process, and students will try anything — eventually!

**The Blues**

"
The students responded to twelve-bar blues very enthusiastically. We let them wear funny hats, and they loved that idea. But, more importantly, musically, they really liked it because they respond well to the beat… We train the drum section to do a very simple rock beat. The kids are just very excited to play along with that kind of rhythm section. It's different than what they've done before. They love the sheer volume of it, because we'll put over 300 kids together for this, and it's just the largest ensemble they've ever played in, so they love that.
"

Michael Jampole, Music Director
Highcrest Middle School
Wilmette, IL

# Foundations for Improvisation

When most people hear the word "improvisation," they think of jazz. Jazz is only one of many genres that features improvisation. Improvisation has been an integral part of Indian classical music for centuries. Some cultures focus the art of improvisation on the ornamentation of the melody, such as in Irish music, while others use the pitch center of the melody as a tonal environment, within which the players create their own musical expression. This can be found in some forms of Spanish Flamenco music.

## Improvisation:

◈ activates a brain hierarchy that favors the ears over the eyes;

◈ redirects the brain from working exclusively off of its memory centers (a style of mental organization that we're expected to constantly articulate in school in order to get good grades), switching into a creative, self-initiating mode;

◈ provides musicians with an opportunity to design their own, original music;

◈ heightens appreciation for the composer's ability to manipulate melodic ideas and structures;

◈ encourages risk-taking, which in turn raises the player's self esteem: "I met the challenge. I did it!";

◈ helps facilitate the development of a clear mental map of the fingerboard. Instead of constantly being engaged in translating dots on a page into muscle moves, the player is involved in seeing and hearing the possibilities within a given key on their fingerboard, aurally and spatially;

◈ enables individuals to create something from nothing — a skill that can be used in all walks of life;

◈ activates original thinking, which can be applied to all facets of life, not just music.

There are at least five foundations you can use to approach improvisation with your students. They are outlined on the following pages:

# 1) Call and Response

Call and response can be used as an extremely effective warm-up to help prepare first-time improvisers. It stimulates the ear-to-instrument hook-up they will need when creating their own melodic lines. Just as there are certain techniques the classical player must master in order to interpret classical literature fluently, improvisers must learn how to hear a musical idea in their inner ear, and be able to externalize that idea on their instrument. This requires a strong foundation in relative pitch, and the ability to recognize pitch as it relates to the layout of their particular instrument.

Ironically, training to improvise boils down to the fact that you have to hear it to play it, but you have to play it to hear it! For instance, if an individual has never played chromatic tones between the scale tones, he or she won't be likely to use them when improvising. In fact, I've found that classically trained musicians' ears have trouble even recognizing that those notes exist. If I play a phrase, like C E F, they won't have a problem finding the notes on their instrument. But if I play C Eb E F, they'll try everything they can think of to find that extra (chromatic) note — usually unsuccessfully. The same is true for rhythmic phrases that incorporate syncopation, odd meter, or asymmetrically repeated notes.

Keeping this in mind, try to introduce lines based on jazz or non-Western scales, chromatic motion, and phrases that vary rhythmically when you lead call and response games.

Call and response can stimulate interval recognition, particularly if you identify the relationships as you go along. For instance, you can play a C to an F, and after everyone has found the two notes, mention that the name of that interval is a perfect fourth. This way, spatial relationships between pitches begin to take on a tangible identity to the ears as well as the mind. They become imprinted as a spatial map in the brain, and a spatial feel within the interrelationships of the fingers, and they get tagged verbally with names. This is a whole-brain learning activity.

---

## "Improv"

Improvisational games and activities create a keener sense of intonation, melodic and rhythmic sophistication, and a window into one's own personal music-making. Improvisation also creates an environment in which humans discover their own compositional abilities. It builds unique personal character, a childlike curiosity about the journey of music; and a profound sense of life participation in music. There is no doubt in my mind, after sixteen years of teaching through my organization, Music For People, that improvisation is one of the great activities that lead people into finding music closer to their soul and more natural to their own way of doing things.

David Darling
Improvising cellist
Founder of Music for People
Goshen, CT

If you feel comfortable with this, you can start by only using the voice. This frees players from technical concerns. Once they've had a chance to work with echoing phrases vocally, then switch them back onto their instruments.

Playing notes and musical phrases in a silent vacuum doesn't really tap into the listening skills required of the improvising musician. I always place call and response into a time and tonal framework by using an accompaniment from a CD or the computer program "Band in a Box." This is because improvisers must be able to simultaneously shape their melodic ideas in relationship to a key, as they conform to meter. If you don't have access to any accompaniments, you can ask several students to create an ostinato (see page 53) against which the rest of the group will practice echoing your phrases back. Build a line over four beats, giving them four beats to echo it back. By limiting them to one measure, they have to stay aware of structure and drop out in time for you to repeat the phrase or create a new one.

## Additive Call and Response

Start by establishing one note; when everyone has found that note, play it back with a second note added in, and then a third, and so on. This gives players' ears a frame of reference as the phrase becomes more complex. Rotate group leadership. Leading a call and response exercise requires thinking in a specific key, remembering the exact melodic/rhythmic phrase so that you can repeat it as many times as is necessary for the group to catch on, and keeping track of time.

## Rhythmic versus Melodic

As we will discuss in the section "Rhythm Games," the control center for pitch in the brain is in a different location than the center for rhythm. Try separating the two when you conduct call and response games by providing more and more complex rhythmic phrases on a single note, and then keeping the rhythmic element fairly bland when providing the group with melodic lines. As group members become more advanced, you can combine the two together.

*Note:* If you don't feel confident in your ability to come up with melodic/rhythmic lines for your students or ensemble, borrow them from music CDs. Make sure they represent different styles so that you are sure to present varied approaches to melodic and rhythmic phrasing.

I've always thought that Mozart was the beginnings of jazz. Jazz is pretty much questions and answers. In Mozart's Marriage of Figaro, for instance, you can hear the call and response. There's this riff with oboes, and they're answered by the flutes, and when I explain this in rehearsals, the flutes and oboes get it. Then I make them improvise around it, which really builds some strong musician skills. Usually, musicians who read don't like to improvise.

I have them transpose the music, and I help them to do this. Because all of my orchestras are mentoring orchestras, I have varying levels of players. Some of them have difficulty transposing—the violins have never done it. When they all do it together, it creates this chaotic sound.

Then they start to realize that the only thing that will hold them together is the rhythm. Pitch and rhythm have close ties, but rhythm is supreme. And in order to keep it together, they have to listen to the other members of the orchestra. It's about learning to listen to what's going on around you. You're playing a part of a piece, and your volume, your pitch, and how you play all depends on your role in the ensemble, and what's going on around you.

Robert Winstin
Metropolis Youth Symphony, Chicago

---

# 2) Drone

A drone is a continuously held pitch. It provides a fixed tonal center that is sounded out as a background accompaniment to the improvisation. The student(s) generating the drone have the opportunity to practice sustaining a note for a long period of time. You can ask them to focus on specific technical concerns or on pure listening while sounding out the drone. The challenge here, is to prevent the mind from wandering, and to listen as carefully as possible.

The soloist has an opportunity to create melodic lines based on a scale of his or her choice. You can focus the improvisations on the development of a melodic theme with variations, or allow the soloist to play freely without any goal other than to try to find notes and/or melodic ideas that they like.

### Example:

Choose a key. Ask the group to hold long tones on the tonic, and give each player an opportunity to improvise over this accompaniment. Soloists can use any type of scale they want. If the group is inexperienced, start with one- or two-note improvisations before branching out into using the full scale.

> When I improvised over the drone, for the first time in my playing years I understood the wonder of improvisation and the sense of freedom one can feel when allowing your own feelings to emerge in a safe environment. I was totally absorbed with my own creation and forgot about the room and others around me. This is what I would call my first experience with meditation. I can understand its power.
>
> Cathy Haines
> Lead Teacher, Orchestra for Cedar Rapids Community School District, Iowa

Here are some sample scales to help you get started:

Found in jazz (mixolydian mode) and used in music from East India:

East Indian, Middle Eastern, Indonesian, Greek:

Found in jazz (lydian mode) and used in music from Africa and East India:

Asian, East Indian, and Middle Eastern:

Found in jazz (lydian dominant scale) and used in music from East India:

East Indian:

East Indian:

East Indian:

Middle Eastern and African:

# PURPOSE

A drone provides a less confining environment for improvisation, because the player doesn't have to be concerned with adhering to the confines of a particular type of scale or rhythmic phrase. Each member of the group can experiment with creating his or her own music without the possibility of "making a mistake"; you can also expose the group to new scales and, therefore, new maps on the instrument.

A drone can also be used as a framework for teaching students to listen more closely to intonation and harmony. You can ask a small group to hold a drone based on the key of a piece from your repertoire, and subgroups or individual musicians can practice its scale or the actual piece, focusing on tuning each pitch to the drone.

# INHERENT CHALLENGES

1) Most musicians will gravitate towards the use of a major or minor scale. Invite them to use other combinations of notes. Introduce them to these sounds by warming up on a scale that originated in a different part of the world. You can use examples from page 52, or from my book, *Planet Musician*, as a reference for world scales.

2) The group will tend to hold the drone too loudly. Try telling the group, "If you can't hear the soloist, then you're playing too loudly." This gives students an opportunity to develop new listening skills.

3) Some individuals (and this occurs with professionals as well as students ) may say, "I don't know what to play." Sometimes coaching the players to "tell a story" helps. If necessary, you can limit them to two or three notes and ask them to create a melody out of those notes, so that they won't feel overwhelmed by the possibilities. If they still can't get started, you can warm them up by playing a three- or four-note melodic idea and asking them to echo it back. They will be using their ears for call and response the same way they need to for improvisation — that is, hearing it first on the inside and then finding it on their instrument.

# 3) Ostinato

An ostinato consists of a short, repeating melodic phrase. For our purposes, it's best to limit the melodic phrase to a three- to six-note melody that is played repetitiously. Unlike the drone, an ostinato offers a tonal _and_ rhythmic environment in which the improviser can explore creative ideas.

Start out by defining the concept of ostinato to the group, and then demonstrate a couple of sample ostinatos. Choose one, and challenge the group to find the notes by ear as you repeat them. This provides a nice warm-up for the ears. Then give each player an opportunity to improvise over this accompaniment. After supplying the group with the first few ostinatos, challenge members to create their own. Give students a few minutes to make up their ostinatos and then have them perform them one at a time. You can either have the group learn one another's ostinatos, so that each soloist is playing over a whole-group accompaniment, or you can ask students to partner up in front of the group and solo over one another's repeating phrases one at a time.

## Ostinato Revisited

Once the players are comfortable inventing their own ostinatos, you can create a multi-layered piece of music, consisting of a series of ostinatos that interlock. This piece can be used as an accompaniment for soloing, or as a piece unto itself. Start with one basic backdrop (something simple, consisting of only two or three notes) and ask each participant to create and extemporaneously layer in a new ostinato that complements the original one. Continue until everyone is playing their ostinato simultaneously. This provides an excellent exercise for pitch and rhythmic training. For instance, if you initiate an ostinato that incorporates syncopation, and you're working exclusively with classically-trained musicians, it may take a number of attempts for each of them to find a phrase they can add that complements yours, because they will have trouble hearing the downbeat within your off-beat phrase.

It's also great to divide the ensemble into groups of two, asking one person to initiate an ostinato while the other one layers in another (spontaneously) without starting and ending in the same place as the first player. This is extremely difficult, because the downbeat of the first ostinato, and the integrity of the melody as it ends, tends to pull one's ears, like a magnet, to mirror the musical phrase.

**Example:**

Here are some sample ostinatos to help get you started. Transpose them into appropriate keys for your group.

## PURPOSE

This is an excellent opportunity for each musician to practice listening in new ways. The ostinato challenges students to figure out the key signature or tonal center and design a complimentary scale with which they can solo. They will also have a chance to interact rhythmically against the ostinato.

## INHERENT CHALLENGES

An ostinato limits the scale tones players can use, because the scale has to fit against the repeating melodic phrase; it also introduces a more rhythmic element to the improvisation than a drone accompaniment does.

1) At first, players may stumble a bit before they find notes that will work against the ostinato. Depending upon the group's ability level, sometimes it's better to hold off on improvisation until the second or third time you do this. While the students become comfortable with the concept, use the ostinato as an ear training exercise. Ask them to identify the rhythms in the phrase, and then challenge them to invent scales that will work with it.

2) You may notice that classically-trained musicians will tend to come up with ostinatos that are fairly symmetrical, rhythmically speaking. Encourage them to use syncopation or to make the phrase more rhythmically interesting. Challenge each member of the group to take the same four notes and place them in different rhythmic structures, in order to open up everyone's minds to new possibilities. You can use the call and response technique, so that the group echoes back each participant's rhythmic idea. If no one in the group is able to shape the phrase in a rhythmically imaginative way, have students echo different rhythmic phrases that you introduce. Then choose the most interesting one and invite each to solo over it.

3) Players will tend to stick to create ostinatos in 4/4 time. Make sure that your examples introduce them to time signatures like 5/4 or 7/8.

# 4) Melody-Based Improvisation

As its name suggests, this approach challenges the players to create an improvisation solely based on the melody. You can use the doubling or tripling of notes; harmonization of the melody; embellishments such as grace notes, turns, slides; and any other instrumental techniques available.

Since it isn't possible to embellish and/or harmonize with a melody unless you know thoroughly it might be better to start with one melodic phrase from your lesson or ensemble music, and experiment with different ways of ornamenting it. You can gradually branch out to larger sections of the piece.

Note: The ensemble must memorize the melody before attempting this approach.

## PURPOSE

While attempting to ornament a melodic line, musicians discover the difference between learning a melody just barely well enough to perform it, and knowing a melody so well that they are able to silently play it by hearing it internally as they simultaneously picture it on their instrument.

This is an excellent time to introduce an analytical view of the piece of music, if you are so inclined. For instance, if I were teaching the tune "Summertime," I might want to point out to students that the opening line starts on the fifth of A minor, moves to its minor third, and follows this by gradually navigating melodically to resolve the phrase on the tonic. This information, if I've taught them the A minor scale and chord tones (1 ♭3 5 ♭7) as a warm-up for improvisation, would enable them to navigate melodic-based improvisation more smoothly.

## INHERENT CHALLENGES

It's tricky to come up with new possibilities on a memorized melody if the melody is only locked into muscle memory. Train your students by asking them to sing a phrase of the melody while naming the notes, and even to attempt first to embellish the melody vocally, before moving on to experimenting with it instrumentally.

If they are still experiencing difficulty, use call and response on the first phrase of the melody, and give them an opportunity to hear/play the phrase with rhythmic variations, grace notes, turns, slides, textural additions, and anything else you can think of. This will help open their imaginations to the possibilities. As you then go around the room and give each student a chance to try this on his or her own, Ask the whole group to echo back each new variation created by students.

**Basic Melody**

**Embellished Melody**

# 5) Descriptional or Illustrative Improvisation

This approach to improvisation uses images to stimulate improvisational ideas. Players can use textures, as well as melodic ideas, to illustrate a visual image or environment (real or imagined). While, it's best at first for the leader to supply the images, you can eventually invite group members to come up with some of their own.

### Example:

Ask group members to illustrate the sounds of a train, a thunderstorm, or a helium balloon being filled and emptied. If they're up to it, try less concrete images, such as a mind thinking, grass growing, or even the inside of a molecule! Try emotions, as well (love, anger, fear, envy...). Invite them to use all accessible materials to make sound, not just their instruments (jingling house keys, tapping on the seat, their voices, etc.)

Since most vocalists and instrumentalists are melodically-oriented in their training, I like to use the following warm-up for this exercise:

### Warmup:

Standing in a circle, ask each participant to demonstrate a textural sound on his or her instrument, and invite the group to echo it back. To get students started, you might suggest typical sounds like trills or slides, and then move on to the sounds of various household items, such as the kitchen blender, the toaster, or a hair-blower. Through imitation, students will discover new sounds on their instruments. Once their imaginations are flowing, try less concrete objects, like a plant growing in the sunlight, or a lightbulb gradually cooling down.

Note: Please refer to Soundstories on page 68 for a more complex approach along these lines.

## PURPOSE

 This exercise helps musicians link their listening, as well as playing abilities, to emotional or experiential content, rather than focusing exclusively on the creation of melodic ideas.

## INHERENT CHALLENGES

If students are unable to get started with this exercise, you can first discuss what each image might sound like. You could also have each person demonstrate one sound they think could describe the image, and then put the sounds together as a group. If students are really shy or embarrassed, use call and response to get them started. Once musicians realize the fun they can have, it's hard to hold them back!

Every year we bring both international players and talented local improvisers together for a week-long event here in Alabama, now famous as the Birmingham Improv Festival. One of the annual highlights of the festival is the Large Improv Orchestra, in which everyone is invited to participate.

We even hand out extra instruments (violins, horns, & percussion) and encourage those in the audience who have never played an instrument or participated in such an extravaganza to choose an instrument and join in. Since they don't know their instrument, they would, of course, be the best improvisers of all! All the musicians arrange themselves according to instrumental families (winds, strings, etc.) and in the initial stage, a conductor will demonstrate a few simple rules to get started, like, "this gesture means solo"; "this gesture means everybody"; or pointing to a section while indicating dynamics, like staccato, legato, or rhythmic "hits."

Once a few parameters are established, everybody joins in the fun! After a few exemplary pieces, we then turn the conducting honors over to new conductors from the group, and folks are really eager to have a hand at it. It's hilarious and exciting to watch the different languages of the body as individuals get up and express their own way of conducting. Never does it fail that each person will have a unique and specific impact on the music and vice versa, as the music impacts the decisions and responses of the conductor.

LaDonna Smith
Editor, The Improvisor
http://www.the-improvisor.com

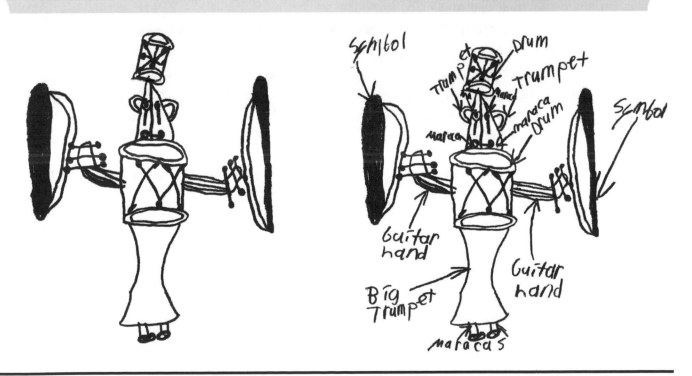

# 6) Harmonic Changes

In folk, Latin, blues and jazz, the key signature only applies to the melody. Once the musician starts to improvise, he or she can build lines out of the chord symbols to create a more sophisticated solo rather than one based on a single scale. Each chord symbol tells the player what key to play in, what type of scale to use, and for how long. You will need to teach your students the primary chord tones (1, 3, 5, 7) and appropriate scale for each chord in the piece.

Think of each chord change like a coded road map; each will guide the ears and fingers into a new tonal center. It's important to emphasize the chord tones of a piece while improvising; they are the pillars of the improvisation. The other notes of the scale are vehicles that carry the player to and away from the chord tones in new and interesting ways.

Pick a tune and, after teaching your students the melody, review the chord and scale tones indicated in the piece. Then encourage each student to practice building an improvisation in which he or she primarily focuses on highlighting the chord tones in varying order, using scale tones like staircases leading in and out of the chord tones.

It's extremely demanding to originate a cohesive melodic idea while asking the brain to pump out road maps for arpeggios and scales in keys that keep changing. This training can take years. The best way to expose classically trained or folk musicians to this for the very first time is to use a simpler form, like a folk or pop tune, the blues, a rock or pop piece, or rhythm changes. Refer to Jamey Aebersold's Music Minus One CDs for accompaniments and instructional books to work with in these genres.

Here's an example of a warm-up you can use on the popular *I IV V I* progression. Ask your students to play the root and third of each key only when they can play the root notes from memory, and know where they are at all times. Then play the root, third, and the fifth, and finally add the (in this case) flatted seventh, moving through the chords in the order of the progression. Play through the progression from the third of each key down to its root. Then start on the fifth of each key, moving through its major third down to the root. Once that is stable, start on the flat seventh of each key, moving down through its chord tones to the root.

Students can also practice inventing short melodic patterns and moving them across the chord progression, as a preliminary step to improvising through the form.

## INHERENT CHALLENGES

Improvisation on chord changes requires the development of whole-brain thinking: the right brain sees a spatial map for each key on the instrument and generates creative ideas; the left brain remembers the chords' names in sequential order; the ears and muscle memory work together to guide the hands. The end product is a harmonically sophisticated solo that is groove-based, fun, and musically interesting. Players will tend to fall back on their strongest skill first. Try to encourage them to reorganize the hierarchy by slowing down and generating notes from a weaker skill (naming or picturing versus hearing or muscle memory).

# Suggested Discography

## Drone

*Didjeridoo: The Australian Aboriginal Music*
Label: Playasound

## Ostinato

*Global Meditation, Volume 3: Percussion - The Pulse of Life*
Track 1: Farafina by Burkina Faso's Farafina
Label: Ellipsis Arts

*Global Meditation, Volume 1: Chant - Voices of the Spirit*
Track 6: Sequences Polyphoniques by Bibayak Pygmies of Gabon
Label: Ellipsis Arts

*Zimbabwe: The Soul of Mbira*
Label: Nonesuch

## Melodic Improvisation

Irish fiddling is a great resource to demonstrate how the same melody can be interpreted many different ways. Browse your local record store and try to find two different artists playing the same tune (such as James Kelly, Martin Hayes, or Kevin Burke).

## Illustrative Improvisation

Music for film or television can be used to demonstrate music that tells a story, or you can play something like "Peter and the Wolf" or "The Sorcerer's Apprentice" for your group. Even though these works don't include improvisation, they are still useful examples.

## Chord Changes

Almost any blues or jazz recording will demonstrate soloing over chord changes.

# GAMES AND TECHNIQUES

# CIRCLE GAMES

ost rooms meant to accommodate groups are organized so that the presenter, teacher, or conductor can make eye contact with every individual. When seated within the group, it's almost considered rude to look around — not that it's easy to see much anyway.

Understandably, musicians are grouped according to instrument and blended based on volume. As justifiable as these seating arrangements are, they can perpetuate a feeling of anonymity and powerlessness. There are musical cultures throughout the world, such as the Balinese Gamelan Orchestra or certain indigenous South American tribes, that favor group consensus. These groups often use a circular seating arrangement.

Placing your group into a circular configuration from time to time (or permanently) during rehearsal will promote a new level of interconnectedness and will influence how players listen to each other. After all, we naturally turn our heads to look when we hear a sound. But the music-stand counters this natural inclination. Once you break "the rules," you may even consider moving around the room, trying out different locations to lead from. In Scandinavia, the leader (the fiddler) stands in the middle of the circle and turns around as he or she provides rhythm and melody. It's also marvelous to turn leadership over to volunteers; you can hear so much more from so many different vantage points when the hierarchy is changed.

The following games have been designed for circular positioning, but you can try any exercise in this book with group members positioned so that they are all equal and in eye contact with one another.

## The Magical Ball

All it takes is one inexpensive tennis or beach ball to make a group forget about feeling self-conscious, create ensemble interaction, stimulate imaginative playing, and have fun in the process.

When working with a group that's new to improvisation, you can pull out a ball, place it on the floor, and kick it to a student in the circle. Ask that student to kick it to someone else, and so on. Let this unfold naturally for a few minutes, and then gradually add in progressively challenging assignments:

1) "Can you kick the ball so that it rolls smoothly right up to the person you've chosen?" (Most students start off by kicking it too hard and it keeps rolling outside of the circle.)

2) "When the ball rolls to you, play three notes of your choice and then kick it to someone new." (Students tend to focus on the ball so much that the notes come easily.)

3) "When the ball reaches you, make the strangest sound you can think of on your instrument and then kick the ball to someone new." (You can move this step into call and response with the group, too, by asking the group to echo back the sound.)

4) "When the ball reaches you, identify something in your home that makes a noise — mechanical or living — and imitate that sound on your instrument. Then kick the ball to someone new." (After four or five students have had a turn at this, challenge the group to echo back sounds created by the next few students, and then invite the group to contribute other musical interpretations.)

This exercise can lead to dividing the students into small groups and sending them off to choose an image, or even create a short story using images, that they will illustrate through sound. They are allowed to plan but not rehearse this. Then they can present their improvisation to the group, and the group can try to guess the image. If you use this technique with a Suzuki group, it's helpful to ask for parent volunteers to coach each group. You can circulate around and eavesdrop or be available to answer questions.

## Example:

A group I worked with at a Suzuki Festival in Massachusetts created an improvisation that described a highway with cars that crashed and bounced up into outer space, and then landed in an airport back on earth. The rest of the group actually guessed correctly, because the improvisation described each location so clearly.

### PURPOSE

This approach to improvisation creates a casual environment that encourages musicians to explore their instruments in new ways. The process fosters ensemble interaction through cooperation.

### INHERENT CHALLENGES

When the students break off into smaller groups, students who have so many ideas that they can't allow others to contribute, or can't make up their minds themselves, can gum up the works. That's where you can help: by showing the students how to process suggestions as a group and make a decision that is agreeable to everyone.

If each member of the group has a different idea and won't agree, you can encourage students to figure out how to integrate all of their ideas into one piece.

# The Group Note

"Pass" a note from player to player around the circle. Each musician should play a single note; it can be a random note selected by the player, or a specific note agreed upon in advance. Let it go around once or twice to observe what happens. Then invite students to try to:

1) make the note move around the circle on a pulse;

2) move the note randomly, allowing it to elongate, shorten, speed up, slow down;

3) "toss" the note across the circle, using eye contact and body movement;

4) move the note through the group on a specific rhythmic phrase without losing a beat;

5) try each of the above with eyes closed.

# Pass the Note

Call for a volunteer conductor. First, ask the players to close their eyes, and tell them that they can play a note of their choosing when they are tapped on the shoulder by the conductor. Once they are warmed up, tell the group that every time someone to their left (or right — your choice) plays a note, they should play an answering note or textural sound. Now they'll play a note when they're either tapped or hear the person next to them play one. As the conductor taps more shoulders, he or she will set more revolutions around the circle from varying start points.

If any individual isn't listening carefully enough — particularly because you've removed visual signals — the motion of the piece will keep stopping when it reaches that player. You can stop and point this out, and then start the piece again. With eyes closed, it's easier for participants to try out new sounds. The group will laugh if anyone plays a particularly weird sound. That's fine. Having fun while learning to listen more carefully and pay closer attention to the ensemble is exactly what we want!

# The Metronome Game

In the introduction to this book, I encouraged you to modify or adapt the exercises presented in this book. Here's one of my "hand-me-down" modifications!

In 1976, my jazz teacher, Sal Mosca, in a desperate attempt to train me to hear and maintain a rhythmic pulse, assigned a clapping exercise. With the metronome set to 60 (60 ticks per minute equals one per second), I was to clap in sets of 10. If I really clapped on the beat, the sound of my clap eclipsed the metronome's click. When I got it right, it sounded as if someone had unplugged the metronome. Most of my claps were early or late for the first few months, though. If you can hear a clap and a tick, even if you can't distinguish which came first, you haven't done it correctly.

Fifteen years later, I was hired to create and present a two-day training workshop at a large utility company, focused on improving team spirit. The following exercise was the hit of the course: it was the only time everyone actually dropped their corporate titles and listened to each other, cheering one another on.

## The Game

Invite the group to stand in a circle. Place a metronome (preferably an electronic one with a loud tick) on a table just outside the circle and set it to 60. Have the group rotate once (clockwise or counter — your call) each time the player standing next to the metronome has clapped however long he or she wants (or you can limit the number of claps). The challenge is to blank out the metronome by clapping exactly on the tick. Few will be able to do it, but group members will listen like they've never listened before — to each other, not just themselves!

# COMPOSER/CONDUCTOR GAMES

iving each of your students an opportunity to lead provides them with a deeper understanding of the role you play, contributes to their skill-base, and therefore, their self-esteem; and helps create a group of leaders rather than followers. It's an interesting way to learn about your own relationship to your group, too. Some of your students may imitate your mannerisms, and others may contribute something totally original that will influence what you do in the future!

## Soundstories

In February 2002, based on a commission by the The Cedar Rapids Symphony Orchestra, my orchestral soundstory, *The Hobo Violin*, premiered. This story features a violinist and her violin as the main protagonists, and was performed by 453 seventh- and eighth-graders. The piece included scores representing a variety of contemporary styles, as well as freely improvised sections designed by the students in workshop to illustrate specific parts of the narrated story.

I designed *The Hobo Violin* with a new prototype in mind for music programs: I would like to see music teachers help their students design their own stories and their own composed, as well as improvised, music.

The Cedar Rapids version was created for second- and third-year string students. The scores included Irish, old time, the blues, and classical with a world jazz tinge. The students had a chance to develop their ideas during two days of rehearsals leading into the dress rehearsal and performance, and they had a chance to act within the piece, which I narrated with help from two students and two faculty members.

## Directions

The orchestral soundstory utilizes improvised textural and melodic ideas, as well as original scores, to tell or enhance a written or extemporaneously-invented story. The story can be based on:

1) a dream shared by someone in the ensemble;

2) a story invented by a member or member(s) of the ensemble;

3) a fable or myth;

4) an historic event (which can be coordinated with the social studies department or be in response to world events); or,

5) a story invented by the leader. The story can be narrated in conjunction with the musical performance, or the group can tell the story through music and the listeners can describe what they pictured while listening.

Once you have chosen or created a story, choose a narrator or narrators, and prepare the group to improvise behind the narration. It's helpful to prearrange the places within the story that will be accompanied by the group, and even to rehearse certain textures or moods, choosing who will play when, so that the whole group isn't playing all of the time. You may choose to conduct students in and out, and indicate volume levels. Or you can select an ensemble member to coordinate or conduct the piece. If you decide to evolve the piece over time, you can even help students compose melodic themes that can be used at key points within the story.

## PURPOSE

 This approach stimulates teamwork, exercises the imagination, and calls for more inventive ways to play one's instrument. It also:

◆ teaches students a number of approaches to improvisation;

◆ introduces students to a number of different musical styles;

◆ provides students with a creative goal;

◆ orients students to search for the intention of each piece of music — whether it's to create a certain type of mood, tell an emotional story, or create an energetic effect on its listeners — rather than always burying themselves in the linear, note-to-note mechanical process of playing a score.

Some groups will plunge in, while others may play too softly or not at all; so make sure that you spend enough time developing the skills necessary for students to feel confident, and to find their way out of fear and into the exhilaration of imagination. You can use  "The Magical Ball" on page 64 to warm them up to this approach.

## Soundstory Revisited

During a performance, you can invite the audience to make up a story, which the musicians then "retell" through sound. I like to get the audience started by saying something like "Once upon a time," and then I fill in the sentence with something and point to someone in the audience to add a sentence or two. I keep pointing to audience members one by one until we have a beginning, middle, and end to the story. Then the fun begins as the musicians interpret what they've heard through sound.

This approach requires tremendous teamwork within the ensemble, as well as good listening skills. It's always fun for both the audience and the ensemble.

---

# Trafficking

The title, "trafficking," describes the role a volunteer leader can play by conducting and composing simultaneously. Since the game doesn't allow physical leadership while the piece is in progress, leaders must learn how to express their musical ideas succinctly and memorably through a verbal description. The game compels them to learn to pay attention to the construction of a successful piece of music: one that has a clear beginning, middle, and end; is original; and provides the group with an interesting foundation out of which they can develop a successful piece of music.

If you have enough time, you can give each ensemble member a chance to compose a piece for the group. In turn, the group will have a succession of opportunities to improvise within a perfectly mistake-free environment that balances structure with freedom. I have used this exercise — modified from one I learned from composer Meyer Kupferman back in 1973 — with groups of all ages. I usually lead the first few pieces before I ask for volunteers. I try to show different styles of leadership (see examples below) during those first few pieces, and always double-check before we start to make sure that everyone remembers what they've been asked to do. The group won't have the opportunity to rehearse. It's fine to review the instructions, but don't write them down.

Set the group up so that members can see each other easily. Using only verbal instructions (without demonstrating or conducting), create a piece of music that has a well-defined beginning, evolution, and ending. The composer will be able to sit down and listen to the performance once he or she has described the part each musician will play in the piece. I've found that musicians can learn a lot about the art of communication when they hear how their words have been interpreted — or misinterpreted — depending upon how they've described the piece. Sometimes it's helpful to discuss this afterwards, leading with questions such as, "Is this what you thought it would sound like?" If it isn't, ask the composer, "How could you have described that differently so that the piece would have sounded closer to what you intended?"

Here are some pieces that groups I've worked with have created. Each piece represents a different style of leadership.

## 1) Sample Piece

In this first piece, individuals in the group were given very specific information about when to enter and how long to play, while the actual pitches, speed, and emotional content were left up to each player:

"John, I'd like you to start the piece by playing spacy music that makes us feel as though we're floating. Tia, after John has created this feel, establish a rhythmic pulse that moves at a medium tempo. Jordan, Rachel, and Will: count to 16 and then play long tones with four counts in between each one. Christopher, once they have played four long tones, begin to improvise over this accompaniment. Stop when you feel like you've played enough. Once he ends his improvisation, everyone should gradually play softer and softer until you've all stopped except for John. John, you end the piece however you want."

## 2) Sample Piece

Here's an example of a piece built out of images:

"Sophie, represent the sounds of a scared squirrel running up a tree and Eugene will be the dog chasing the squirrel. When Teressa makes the sounds of rain, Eugene and Sophie drop out. Then I'd like all of the horn players to make the sounds of thunder, starting really loud and getting quieter and quieter until you fade away. Then the flutes will play a melodic solo that sounds like the clouds slowly blowing away. And then the dog will chase the squirrel again. The piece will end when the dog howls."

## 3) Sample Piece

This piece uses musical conductors to move it along:

"Kara, stand up and play a slow pulse on your oboe. Use an 'A' note. Group One, when she nods at you, play lyrical lines using the notes 'A,' 'B,' and 'D' in any order you wish. Liz, after they have established the introduction, stand up and use your cello rhythmically, nodding group number two in on your rhythmic phrase. Group Two, you can only tap, clap, or click — no melodic lines. David, use your flute to point to players from group number three for solos. Point them in and then point them out. When David points at any one of you, Group Three, you must create a melodic line over the background. Everyone, when Kara sits down, the piece will fade out."

In time you can refine the pieces, experimenting with visual images, stories, or other modes of communication, such as communicating melodies or rhythmic feels by singing them to members of the group for use in the piece. You may wish to use your whole body to act out the feel of the piece. You can create performable pieces out of the ideas that are developed. During a performance, you may even challenge someone in the audience to volunteer to lead a piece. Improvisational actors have included audience participation for years. Why not musicians?

# PURPOSE

Inventing a sequence of musical events that is cohesive and interesting helps develop the ability to perceive and create integral structures. Group members have a chance to exercise their memorization skills rather than stare at sheet music, and once the piece is in motion, everyone has to listen to one another carefully — something that doesn't always occur when reading music. This approach also enables the participants to practice their improvisatory skills without the burden of "making mistakes."

# INHERENT CHALLENGES

The group may be reticent to volunteer, at first. Once you get rolling, though, everyone generally wants to try leading the ensemble. Sometimes, someone will volunteer with great enthusiasm, only to blank out when they face the group. That person may be paralyzed by the endless possibilities, or fearful of not doing a good job. Let volunteers know that nothing can go wrong. Offer guidance by whispering suggestions to them, and commending them on the decisions they make. You can also provide some structure within this exercise by offering a starting image or story.

When players get a taste of the power and the fun, and hear the fruits of their creativity, they don't want to stop. The possibilities are endless.

# RHYTHM GAMES

Melody without rhythmic definition would be food without taste. Many forms of early music evolved out of chant and recitative, in which pitch was subservient to the rhythmic shape of the phrase. Almost all styles of music worldwide were originally conceived as integral to either spiritual worship, dance, or both. Music as sheer entertainment — rather than for ritual, or celebration, or as a record of history — developed later. In music classes, we tend to focus on teaching the basic rhythms and how to translate symbols on a page into correctly-measured responses. We tend to extrapolate the heart of music into technically precise muscular movements without connection to its source. Do we still hear and feel the heartbeat? Do we feel the dance? Do we tell the story? Do we connect with our ancestry? For the most part, unfortunately not.

We are enveloped in life's rhythms. The pulse of our heart, the circadian rhythms of our brain, blood pumping through our veins, the monthly rhythms of our hormones, the rise and fall of our temperature — rhythm is life-sustaining. Encourage your students to notice their daily rhythms: the ebb and flow of their energy, the practices they perform at certain times of day such as brushing their teeth, eating, or sleeping. Help them notice how almost all of their daily rituals employ rhythm.

When you teach rhythmic patterns, try not to approach students in an academic (intellectual) way at first. If you ask half the group to stomp on the downbeat, as if squashing an ant, and the other half to clap in between as if they are killing a mosquito, you will bring the "and" of the beat into a feeling of purposefulness (although I invite you to find less morbid images). Try teaching your students to perform a Native American or African rain dance. Give them hand drums or teach them a chant to learn the underlying pulse, and accompanying layers of rhythmic patterns. If you don't have access to authentic resources, you can even invent your own rhythmic chant. ("I love va-ca-tion" or "Ev-ery-bo-dy eat some cho-co cho-co-late!") This approach will provide them with a physical and contextual experience that will give them an important point of reference for learning rhythmic patterns.

We've all had the experience of getting together with a group of people — whether they were our family, a community group, or a musical group — and feeling "out of sync." Then, something occurred to unify us and we found our way into a group connection that uplifted our energies, leaving us exhilarated. As individuals, we'd each given up our personal tempo and found or created a group rhythm.

Rhythm is a language. It unifies large groups of people, whether they are musicians or not. Community drumming circles have become extremely popular throughout the United States for this reason. Throughout history, in every culture, tribes or communities have gathered together to sing or to drum on a regular basis. Why does almost every religion or form of spiritual worship in the world include group singing or chanting? Why isn't it enough to just sit in silence?

When we pause to examine the experiences that give us a sense of belonging and connection to other people or to God, we see that elements of music provide almost every opportunity we have. Rarely silence. The preacher speaks with music in his or her voice; an inspiring speaker creates a passionate, rhythmic build. Even at a sports game, when the crowd roars, it's a variation on tribal singing: a point of view connecting a large group of people through sound. Like placing an autistic child in a bathtub filled with body-temperature water to help the child journey beyond his or her internal world, music weaves groups together, whether they are seated in the audience or participating within the performance group.

## Pitch Versus Rhythm

It has been scientifically determined that the part of the brain responsible for recognizing and duplicating pitch is in a different location than the part that recognizes and duplicates rhythm. In most Western musicians (except percussionists), the part of the brain responsible for pitch is much stronger. It is the same with parts of the brain as it is with limbs: the dominant or stronger muscle (or, in this case, area), will always dominate the weaker muscle or area.

# Strengthening the "Rhythm Muscle"

If you have one leg that you tend to lean on and use more, and you go to the gym and use an exercise machine that requires both legs, the stronger leg will always take over, perpetuating the hierarchy. When it comes to improvisation, the instrumentalist's stronger brain center (pitch), will tend to dominate the weaker one (rhythm), except in the case of drummers or percussionists. Western music tends to be more melody-based, and the rhythms are usually perceived as servants to the melodic motion of the piece. In areas of the world like Cuba, Brazil, or India, rhythmic training is much more intense and complex. Musicians tend to train their pitch and rhythm centers equally. So, how can we train our rhythmic capability in order to equalize our skills? Isolate that "muscle" and work it out on its own!

Look around your classroom or rehearsal space. It's filled with common objects, such as desk drawers that can be opened and closed rhythmically, pens and pencils that can be tapped, keys that can be jangled, and books that can be thumped. Include these objects, in addition to your ensemble's instruments, as you explore rhythmic warm-ups. For instance, a string player can tap on the body of the instrument; horn players can click their keys; pianists can open the top of the piano and play the strings like a harp, or gently thump on them with the palms of their hands; and so on. Here are some other ways to exercise the rhythm muscle:

1) Turn the group into a percussion ensemble;

Play a recording of African drumming and afterwards, extract one of the basic rhythms from the recording, using it as a basis for a spontaneous group piece. Invite each player to layer in his or her own rhythm until the whole group is drumming.

2) Use an ostinato as a basis for improvisation (see page 53);

When we work with an ostinato, even some of the most advanced professional players and teachers can have difficulty switching from the role of melodist to that of the rhythm keeper. After years spent relying on a rhythmic pulse from external sources, they must now learn to originate and maintain the pulse themselves. In that sense, introducing the use of ostinato to instrumentalists and vocalists provides extremely useful rhythmic training.

3) Use call and response for rhythmic phrases;

Before playing new rhythmic lines, it's helpful to use call and response by singing the rhythm or tapping it out. Then start at a slow tempo, increasing the tempo only when everyone is ready.

Here are some rhythmic phrases you can refer to:

# Physicalizing the Beat

If you teach rhythm by encouraging your students to "physicalize" the beat, you are helping your students integrate the motion of the pulse into their bodies as well as their ears. The following rhythmic exercises not only develop listening and audiation skills, but also lead to a physical experience of the beat. This is because time is a spatial event and feeling the pulse is highly beneficial to the learning process.

1) Bounce the rhythmic pulse;

Keep some Swiss exercise balls on hand. Put on a recording of music or ask a part of the ensemble to play a piece from your repertoire. Place the "rhythmically challenged" students on the balls, asking them to bounce the pulse on the ball — it works like a charm!

2) Toss a ball in time to the rhythmic pulse;

Put on a recording and ask the ensemble to throw and catch the ball on the beat.

3) Walk the rhythm;

Invite the group to walk the quarter note in a circle or in place as they clap rhythmic phrases that you or a selected leader provide.

4) Tap the rhythms on each other;

Ask the group to sit or stand in a circle facing the back of the person next to them, and ask someone to tap a rhythmic phrase on the back of the person in front of them; let the group gradually pass the rhythm around the circle. Then choose a new leader to send a new rhythmic phrase around the circle.

Each new leader has to create a rhythmic phrase, and then remember it. The rest of the group is engaged in rhythmic ear training, but they are also physically feeling what they hear.

5) Speak the rhythms;

Finding words that capture and define a rhythmic phrase is a helpful tool when challenged by new combinations. We all know the trip-o-let trip-o-let routine for triplets. Or "good-and-plen-ty good-and-plen-ty" for sixteenths. If you extract a longer phrase from a piece of music and ask group members to invent a sentence that expresses that phrase, it will strengthen their ability to play the phrase correctly in the future.

# Tuning the Interval Clock

I have a student who starts to pack up his violin five minutes before the end of his lesson because he earns his living as a therapist, and is so attuned to the fifty-five minute hour that he does this unconsciously. When I say, "Where are you going?" he looks at the clock in surprise, realizing that he is about to cheat himself out of the last five minutes of his lesson.

In 1998, *The New York Times* published an article by Sandra Blakeslee, discussing a special clock in the brain that tracks time. She cited examples of ways in which we apply this clock, including how the basketball player learns to dribble the ball within an allowable time allotment without looking at the clock or counting. Think of the chef who must track the timing of numerous meals simultaneously.

Ask your students to scan their lives and come up with other examples of how they use this inner clock. For instance, I don't need an alarm clock in the morning; I wake up at whatever time I've chosen the night before. And two weeks before daylight savings time, my system adjusts in anticipation. Truly great jazz musicians can step outside when someone is soloing, have a conversation, and reappear on the bandstand in time for their solo at just the right moment. They no longer need to count the 32-bar structure of the jazz tune being performed. To fine-tune the inner clock, try these exercises with your students:

1) Since our species defines time according to the motion of the second-hand of a clock, how about asking your group to close their eyes and play one note on their instrument until they think 60 seconds has passed by (without counting). Keep your watch in view, and hit a gong or whatever you have on hand when 60 seconds has actually passed to show them how well they did or didn't do.

2) Play a recording of music and ask students to focus on hearing groups of four measures at a time without counting. Focus their ears on the natural conversational tone of the music as it travels over time. Then choose a world music recording that doesn't base its music on the Western groups of four and eight, and ask them to identify the groupings (Indian music often uses odd meters, or you could play a piece of South American folk music, which tends to be rooted in 3/4.)

3) Divide the group in half. Ask one group to play quarter notes for four bars (any pitches they want) and rest for four bars; ask the second group to play quarter notes for four bars in alternation. Tell students to start by counting out the beats, and then ask them to stop counting and to feel how these groupings sit over a certain length of time.

# One Minute Improvisations:

Berry Gordy, founder of Motown Records, created hit after hit because he believed that a song should be like an abbreviated novel. If words tell the story from the brain, then doesn't music tell the story of the heart?

In the early nineties, while working in California, I invited pianist, composer, and author Allaudin Mathieu to play with me for a radio interview on a local public station. We had extra time after the interview and performance of the rehearsed piece of music, so he suggested that we play some freely improvised one-minute improvisations. I have borrowed and modified this suggestion ever since because it's an incredibly direct route to stimulating awareness of the integrity of structure.

When you only have one minute to create a successful piece of music, you automatically orient yourself to creating a succinct introduction, exposition of the idea, and conclusion.

Start your students on learning to play for 60 seconds at a time by asking the whole group to play:

1) a drone;

2) a repetitive idea.

In small sub-groups, come around the room and invite each group to create:

1) a textural improvisation (no melody, just textures) for one minute;

2) a melodic improvisation;

3) a rhythmic improvisation;

4) an improvisation that tells a story (you may prepare them for this by introducing the use of images, for instance: describe a thunderstorm, create a day in the life of a flower, and so on).

These exercises provide students with a wonderful opportunity to explore different musical elements while maintaining an awareness of duration. You are also enabling the group to hear the difference between a contemplative piece of music and one that tells a story.

# Rhythm-Talk

As we discussed earlier, call and response is an effective tool to get a group warmed up and working together. Ask your players to stand up without their instruments, and provide them with a rhythmic phrase shaped over four beats, giving them four beats to echo it back. You can vary the methods by which they respond, to get their blood flowing: you can use gibberish vocalizations, clap it, stomp it, walk it, talk it, sing it, tap it — or any other method you can conceive! If you don't hear group consensus, send them the same phrase again. When the group responds cohesively, try a new one. Gradually, turn leadership over to various individuals in a game of tag. Whoever gets tapped on the shoulder takes over. Try to do this without losing a beat. If you don't feel comfortable initiating rhythmic phrases, prepare ahead of time by selecting some from my book *Planet Musician*, or any world music CD. The recording company *Ellipsis Arts* has created a wonderful archive of music from around the world.

I've found that you can convert a disconnected group of musicians into a tight-knit ensemble in just minutes using this warm-up.

During a rehearsal, you can choose a piece from your ensemble's repertoire and try using the rhythm-talk exercise to help master each challenging rhythmic phrase within the piece. Try this on one pitch, ideally the tonal center of the piece of music. Once the group can competently echo it back, add the actual melodic line that's linked to that rhythmic phrase. You can also ask each section to clap, tap, or vocalize the rhythms of a whole section or piece of music before they attempt to add in the pitches.

# HANDOUTS

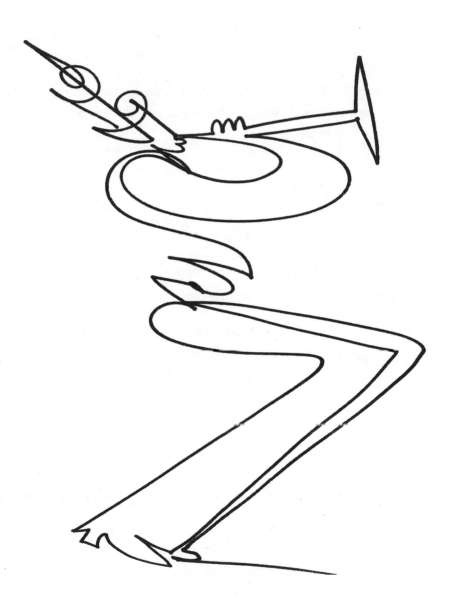

# Playing Healthy Handouts

The following handouts can be copied as many times as you like. They can be handed out to your students or to their parents, depending on the age group.

While we all have busy agendas with our ensembles, if musicians don't pay attention to the effects of repetitive muscle use, they can easily injure themselves and have to lay off from playing altogether. In fact, we're seeing tendinitis and carpal tunnel syndrome appear in younger and younger populations because of repetitive use of the hands and arms at the home computer.

Use the suggested resources and illustrations on the following pages to help you discuss the handouts when you present them to your group. For instance, define the following terms by demonstrating and then asking students to imitate you:

◆ the difference between bad and good posture;

◆ the difference between a flexed or extended wrist and a straight one;

◆ shallow breathing versus deep breathing;

◆ exercises that raise the heart rate, exercises that are meant to strengthen the muscles, and exercises meant to stretch muscles;

◆ how to apply a hot washcloth to an area that's tight or painful, giving a light massage through the washcloth, followed by the application of ice;

◆ how to apply ice by moving it in a circular manner over the entire area;

◆ what signs to look for (such as chronic pain) to address or prevent injury;

Teach players the basics:

◆ Show them that their finger muscles are located in the forearm, not the hand;

◆ Illustrate how a flexed or extended wrist can make it more difficult for the tendons to articulate the fingers by having them pretend they are typing using first a straight wrist, then a flexed wrist, and then an extended wrist;

◆ Encourage them to shift their weight and move around a little bit as they play to avoid a static position that can overload a targeted group of muscles;

◆ If you see a student sitting or standing with bad posture or a locked body position give an image to correct the posture, rather than saying, "Michael, sit up straight." Images such as "reach the top of your head for the ceiling," or, "pretend you have a bright light on your upper chest and try to shine it out across the room," can facilitate better changes than reprimands.

It's also important to structure care for the muscles during rehearsals. For instance, you can instill good habits by scheduling breaks that are constructive (versus only a bathroom or beverage break):

◆ Shake out hands and arms;

◆ Use techniques described in other sections of this book (such as vocal call and response or clapping the rhythms of the selected piece of music) to provide a physical break from playing, yet still work on the music;

◆ Stand up and sit down repetitively to get the blood flowing;

◆ Sway side to side;

◆ Incorporate postural exercises from the reference materials recommended below;

◆ March in place.


If you don't feel confident in your ability to help your musicians in this manner, you can use the following resources to either help train yourself or show to the group:

*You Are Your Instrument:*
*The Definitive Musician's Guide To Practice and Performance*
by Julie Lyonn Lieberman (152-page reference book)

*The Instrumentalist's Guide To Fitness, Health, and Musicianship*
with Julie Lyonn Lieberman (60-minute video)

*The Vocalist's Guide To Fitness, Health, and Musicianship*
with Julie Lyonn Lieberman (60-minute video)

*Violin in Motion*
with Julie Lyonn Lieberman (60-minute video)

**Slumped Posture**

**Hyperextended Posture**

**Aligned Posture**

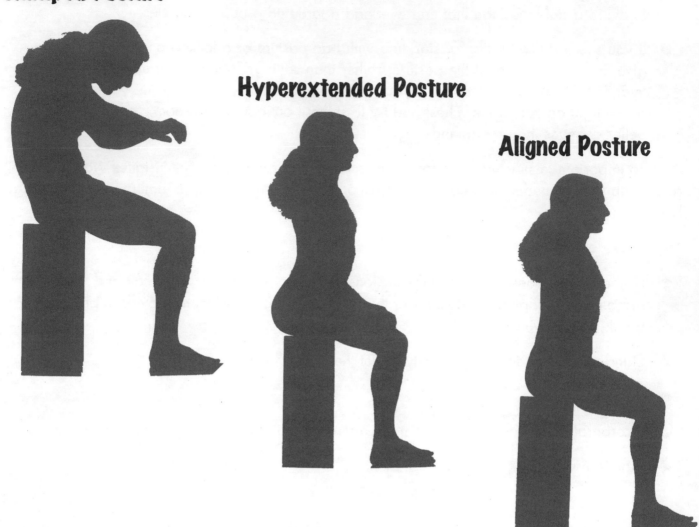

**Flexed Wrist**

**Extended Wrist**

**Aligned Wrist**

# PLAYING HEALTHY
## Julie Lyonn Lieberman: The Creative Band and Orchestra

### Music-Stand Position
Look straight ahead. Leave your head in that position and lower your eyes half-way: the music-stand should be placed so that the music is right there, waiting for you.

### General Posture
Always try to bring the instrument to you instead of turning your body into a pretzel to go to the instrument!

### Standing Posture
Tilt your head back; tilt it down; turn it to the right; turn it to the left. Now come back to center and do your best to keep your head and neck centered when you play.

Lift your shoulders up high and squeeze them up until they feel tired; then relax them down and leave them there!

Stand on or put pressure on your left foot, repeat this with your right, place equal pressure on both feet, and stay there. It's fine to move your feet to new positions as you play — just make sure that your weight is placed equally over both feet.

### Seated Posture
Cross one leg over the other. Now switch to the opposite side. Notice that it's harder to sit up straight with your legs crossed. Now put both feet around to the back of the chair on the right side; do this to the left side. Try to sit up straight in either of those positions! Now bring your feet center with plenty of space between your knees, and put both feet on the floor. You have just found the position that gives support to a nice straight back.

Stick your chest and stomach way, way forward so that you look like a big puff ball, and count to ten. Pull your chest and stomach way, way back so that you are curved over like an empty bowl, and count to ten. Now sit tall and try to balance there without tension while you play.

### Wrist Position
Hold your arms in front of you as if you are about to place your palms on an imaginary wall in front of you and flex your hands up towards you; now extend your wrists by lowering your palms towards the floor; return to neutral (straight wrist) and relax your arms into playing position; try to maintain this alignment in your wrists when making music.

### Constructive Rest
When we practice we need to take little breaks to relax our muscles, check our posture, and get ready to begin again with greater relaxation. Every five or ten minutes, stop, take a deep, deep breath; shake your fingers, your hands, your arms, and then your whole body. Take another deep breath and check your posture before you continue your practice session.

## — JulieLyonn.com —

# PLAYING HEALTHY
## Julie Lyonn Lieberman: The Creative Band and Orchestra

### The most common causes of injury are:

◆ bad posture;

◆ a flexed or extended wrist: try to keep it aligned (straight);

◆ excessive contraction in fingers (tension caused by clenching or pressing down too hard);

◆ emotional effort ("to be good," "to get it," or "to play fast") rather than pure listening and creating with respect for present ability with gradual expansion into speed and complexity;

◆ excessive hours of practice without warm-up/cool-down.

### How you "feed" your muscles will determine their health and stamina.
### Healthy muscles are created by giving them:

◆ oxygen: breathe deeply;

◆ heightened circulation: aerobic exercise;

◆ muscle balance: exercises that use the muscles counter to how they are used when you make music;

◆ Balanced Diet: 8 glasses of water a day; 50% vegetables and fruits; vitamins: Vitamin C, calcium/magnesium, and B complex; while avoiding foods that rob your muscles of nutrition such as: sugar, coffee, processed flour, and soda.

### The healing process must include:

◆ technique rehabilitation (remove the cause of the injury by adjusting how you hold and play your instrument);

◆ rest: practice in small increments; if chronic pain persists, take a few days off;

◆ body-work: massage, acupuncture, hot/cold compresses, castor oil packs, magnets, etc.;

◆ muscle balance: strengthen the opposing and surrounding musculature to give greater support to the injured area;

◆ warm-up/cool-down: never play without stimulating circulation to warm up your muscles; always take the time to shake out and stretch afterwards to lessen the degree of possible problems caused during practice.

— JulieLyonn.com —

# The Creative Practice Session
## Julie Lyonn Lieberman: The Creative Band and Orchestra

Without guidance, a child has no idea what amount of effort will yield what kind of results. Your expectations — with the guidance of the teacher — and your support, will increase his or her progress significantly. Through practicing on a musical instrument, your child has the opportunity to develop spatial, mathematical, and listening skills, mental stamina, fine motor control, and pride in his or her accomplishments.

As with anything, when a parent becomes involved too closely the wrong way, the opposite results can be created. Children already have homework. We have an opportunity at home to make sure that time on an instrument doesn't becomes just one more task before the child can finally have some fun. If discipline around music-making becomes about doing something distasteful on a regular basis because it's supposed to be good for us at some point in the future, the child will eventually lose interest or develop a muted relationship with the instrument.

Practice time can be a time of sharing and bonding rather than yet one more area when they hear you say, "Johnny, did you practice yet?" Your participation in the practice sessions can create quality family time. Clearly you, as a parent, are overwhelmed with professional and domestic responsibilities in addition to parenting, but even once a week is better than not at all.

Here are some suggestions that will help you make a difference:

You can start or end each practice session with an improvisation. Ask your child to describe an image in sound. What does a zipper sound like? How about a train traveling from far away right into the backyard? You can use dreams: "Describe a dream you had this week, and then try to describe it without words by making sounds on your instrument." You can ask your child to write a story and illustrate it with music.

To practice a new technique, challenge your child to use the technique correctly for the amount of time it will take for a wind-up toy to walk across the room, the sands of a minute-glass to run out, or the time it takes the dog or cat to eat his or her dinner!

Sing a note and ask your child to find it on the instrument. If you play an instrument, play a phrase from a piece your child has just started to work on and ask him or her to figure it out by ear.

Try to turn all of the exercises into games rather than work, and your child will learn that consistent playing time, while having fun, can create success.

# Creating The Ideal Practice Environment
## Julie Lyonn Lieberman: The Creative Band and Orchestra

The practice environment that you and your child create, can have a strong effect on your child's rate of improvement, the safety of the instrument, and the development of excellent postural habits. Here are some ideas to help you start to establish a fun, supportive space within which your child can improve.

## Creative and Fun

Think about the environments that tend to make your child feel excited and happy. Try to bring these elements into the practice room. For instance, if your child has a favorite movie, you can mount posters or toys associated with the movie, presenting a new one each time a personal goal is met. If he or she loves animals, you may decorate the practice space with stuffed animals and pictures of animals. If your child loves to draw, mount his or her drawings, or include posters by favorite artists. Into sports? Mount sports cards, posters, and even sports equipment.

## Comfortable

If pain or discomfort is associated with practice, your child will be less likely to be drawn to spending time on their instrument. Make sure that:

1) A bright light is either attached to the music-stand or placed nearby to illuminate the music;

2) The music-stand height can be adjusted to support good posture; ask your child to stand (or sit) in a comfortable position and adjust the stand until the music is directly in their line-of-sight;

3) Establish practice intervals using a clock, a timer, or an hour-glass; encourage your child to take a short break whenever muscles feel uncomfortable and schedule specific activities into the break: shake out the hands and arms for a minute, walk around, or stretch. If you are specific, he or she won't interpret a break as a break from discipline. Instead, the break will establish continuity with the development of discipline through consciously varied uses of the practice session.

# Creating The Ideal Practice Environment
## Julie Lyonn Lieberman: The Creative Band and Orchestra

## Privacy

Over the years, I've heard many student musicians describe how difficult it is to practice in the midst of siblings watching television, family arguments, or negative comments floating in from adjoining rooms. Unless you are specifically coaching or helping your child during their practice session (using positive comments to reinforce good deeds), and giving him or her your undivided attention while doing so, a comment from afar can keep attention diverted to outside of the practice space rather than focused on technique or on listening to the music. Try to keep your comments positive and supportive, and restrict them to the end of the session if you are in another room while they are practicing.

Learning to play an instrument requires subtle motor coordination and self-confidence. Visual and listening skills must be coordinated within time constraints. This requires deep concentration.

A separate room is the best option for practice, but if that isn't possible, even a partition like a folding screen or a curtain hung from the ceiling to the floor can help define the practice space. "A room of one's own," to quote author Virginia Wolf, offers respect and makes the statement, "This is something that's all yours, and we respect you and support your efforts."

## Safety and Organization

The habits a young person develops around care for the instrument and organization of practice materials can play a viable role in contributing to success in all areas of life. Sometimes parents assume that there's no need to address this issue because the instrument may not be of value since it's student quality. Keep in mind that the habits formed around the care for the very first instrument tend to establish a child's regard for material possessions, and establish habits that will transfer to future instruments as well.

1) Place the instrument in a safe place when not in use, and always put it down in that same, safe place when taking a break;

2) Always put the instrument away in its case when practice is finished for the day.

Often, the child comes to depend on the parent to remember things for him or her. This isn't conducive to building important and necessary skills. A good place to begin, is with the materials needed for band or orchestra practice, or for the lesson. Try making a poster or using a blackboard to make a list. Give your child stickers or something else that's fun, which can be used to check off the list when preparing to leave the house.

## Rewarding and Inspirational

When the practice space offers visual evidence of all that's been accomplished so far, as well as future goals, students are constantly reminded of their ability to make progress, and of what they need to focus on next.

Using either a bulletin board, chalk board, or large pieces of paper that are attached to the walls, children can keep a running tally or chart on how many days in a row they've practiced and for how long. There are a number of ways you can design this. If you're planning to give them a reward for specific agreements fulfilled, you can place a picture of the reward at the end of a certain number of days. Make this fun! They can place a sticker or star on the board, or a balloon in the room, for each day they practice. Colors can signify the amount of time.

Inspirational quotes can be posted around their practice space, including positive comments from you or their teacher, as well as things people they respect have said about success. Cross over fields. These quotes don't have to come from musicians. They can come from movie or sports heroes, too.

When friends come to visit, this space will elicit comments that will make your child feel proud of his or her commitment to music.

## Goals

Ask your child to think of some personal goals and then help him or her mount them in full sight. Also include the music teacher's requests.

## Photographs

Try mounting photos in the practice space of your child performing, taking a lesson, rehearsing, or practicing (particularly when he or she is holding the instrument correctly).

# Directory

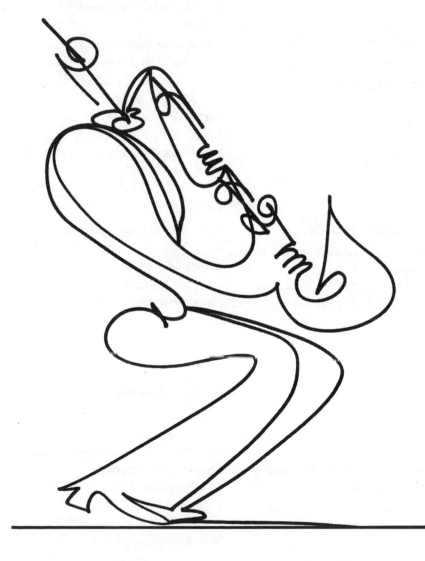

# Directory of Organizations

## American Choral Directors Association

ACDA promotes excellence in choral music through performance, composition, publication, research, and teaching.

**www.acdaonline.org**
502 SW 38th Street
Lawton Oklahoma 73505
Tel.: 580-355-8161
Fax: 580-248-1465

## The American Music Conference

AMC is dedicated to promoting the importance of music, music-making and music education to the general public.

**www.amc-music.org**
5790 Armada Drive
Carlsbad, CA 92008
Tel: 760-431-9124 or 800-767-6266
Fax: 760-438-7327

## American Music Therapy Association, Inc.

The American Music Therapy Association strives to advance public awareness of the benefits of music therapy and increase access to quality music therapy services.

**www.musictherapy.org**
8455 Colesville Road
Suite 1000
Silver Spring, MD 20910
Tel: 301-589-3300
Fax: 301-589-5175
E-mail: info@musictherapy.org

## The American String Teachers Association with the National School Orchestra Association

ASTA with NSOA promotes excellence in string and orchestra teaching and playing.

**www.astaweb.com**

4153 Chain Bridge Road
Fairfax, VA 22030
Tel: 703-279-2113
Fax: 703-279-2114

## The American Symphony Orchestra League

This organization provides leadership and service to American orchestras, while communicating to the public the value and importance of orchestras and the music they perform.

**www.symphony.org**
33 West 60th Street, 5th Floor
New York, NY 10023-7905
Tel: 212-262-5161
Fax: 212-262-5198
E-mail: league@symphony.org
Washington Headquarters E-mail:
heatherw@symphony.org

## Association of Concert Bands

ACB encourages and fosters adult concert community, municipal, and civic bands, while promoting the performance of the highest quality traditional and contemporary literature for band.

**www.acbands.org**
6613 Cheryl Ann Drive
Independence, OH 44131
Tel: 800-726-8720

## Bands of America

A presenter of music events for high school band students, BOA provides "positively life-changing" experiences for students, teachers, parents and communities.

**www.bands.org**
526 Pratt Ave. North
Schaumburg, IL 60193
Tel: 847-891-2263 or 800-848-BAND
Fax: 847-891-1812

## The Commission Project

The Commission Project fosters creativity in education by bringing students together with professional composers and performers.

**www.tcp-music.org**
500 Panorama Trail
Rochester, NY 14625-1848
Tel: 716-385-6440
Fax: 716-385-6441
E-mail: ncorman@tcp-music.org
Contact: Ned Corman

## The Foundation Center

The nation's authority on institutional philanthropy, The Foundation Center is dedicated to serving grantseekers, grantmakers, researchers, and the general public.

**www.fdncenter.org**
79 Fifth Avenue/16th Street
New York, NY 10003-3076
Tel: 212-620-4230, 800-424-9836
Fax: 212-807-3677

## The Grammy Foundation

The GRAMMY® Foundation, a non-profit arm of the Recording Academy, strives to bring national attention to the value of music and arts education.

**www.grammy.com**
3402 Pico Boulevard
Santa Monica, CA 90405
Tel: 310.392.3777
E-mail: info@grammyfoundation.org

## International Association of Jazz Educators

IAJE's mission is to assure the continued, worldwide growth and development of jazz and jazz education.

**www.iaje.org**
P.O. Box 724
Manhattan, KS 66505
Tel: 785-776-8744
Fax: 785-776-6190
E-mail: info@iaje.org

## Jazz at Lincoln Center

Jazz at Lincoln Center is a not-for-profit arts organization committed to promoting the appreciation and understanding of jazz through performance, education, and preservation.

**www.jazzatlincolncenter.org**
33 West 60 Street
New York, NY 10023
Tel: 212-258-9800

## Living Music

Paul Winter's workshops in improvisation are truly spectacular!

**www.livingmusic.com**
Earth Music Productions, LLC
P.O. Box 72/P.O. Box 68
Litchfield, CT 06759
Tel: 860-567-8796
Fax: 860-567-4276
info@livingmusic.com
Contact: Paul Winter

## MENC: The National Association for Music Education

Comprised of 90,000 music educators, university faculty and researchers, college students preparing to be teachers, high school honor society members, and MusicFriends, MENC encourages the study and making of music by all.

**www.menc.org**
1806 Robert Fulton Drive
Reston, VA 20191
Tel: 800-336-3768
Fax: 703-860-4000

## Music for People

Music for People is a grass-roots organization dedicated to re-vitalizing music making for individuals and groups and to promoting music as a means of self-expression.

**www.musicforpeople.org**
187 Sherbrook Dr., Box 397
Goshen, CT 06756 USA
Tel: 877-44MUSIC or 860-491-3763
Fax: 860-491-4513
Contact: David Darling, Artistic Director

## Music from the Heart

This organization offers individual work on improvisation for self-expression, and consults for groups when requested.

2408 Soper Ave.
Baldwin, NY 11510
Tel: 516-623-0663
E-mail: oceansky@optonline.net
Contact: Jim Oshinsky, Emily Metcalf

## Music Teachers National Association

MTNA is committed to furthering the art of music through programs that encourage and support music teaching, performance, composition, and research.

*www.mtna.org*
441 Vine St., Ste. 505
Cincinnati, OH 45202-2811
Tel: 513-421-1420, 888-512-5278
Fax: 513- 421-2503

## NAMM, The International Music Products Association

NAMM is the international voice of the music products industry.

*www.namm.org*
5790 Armada Drive
Carlsbad, CA 92008
Tel: 800-767-6266, 760-438-8001
Fax: 760-438-7327

## The National School Boards Association

This organization promotes excellence and equity in public education through school board leadership.

*www.nsba.org*
1680 Duke Street
Alexandria, VA 22314
Tel: 703-838-6722
Fax: 703-683-7590
E-mail: info@nsba.org

## New Song Library

The New Song Library is a unique song resource library that collects and preserves songs about people's lives, hopes and struggles, and helps performers, teachers and community activists share these songs with a wide variety of audiences.

*http://users.rcn.com/johanna.massed/*
P.O. Box 295
Northampton, MA 01061
Tel: 413-586-9485
E-mail: johanna@massed.net
Contact: Johanna Halbeisen, Executive Director

## Opus 118 - Harlem School for Strings

The Opus 118 Music Center was founded in 1991 on the belief that music education, being the right of every child, must be an integral part of public school.

*www.opus188.org*
P.O. Box 986
New York, NY 10029
Tel: 212-831-4455
Fax: 212-831-5155
Email: Opus 118NY@aol.com

## People's Music Network for Songs of Freedom and Struggle

This organization is made up of a network of musicians, performers, songwriters, recording engineers, record producers, and music lovers who use music and culture to promote progressive ideas and values.

*http://peoplesmusic.tripod.com*
Tel: 914-626-4507
1150 Berme Road
Kerhonkson, NY 12446
E-mail: pmnsfs@hvi.net
Contact: Sarah Underhill

## School Band and Orchestra

School Band and Orchestra is a magazine for school band and orchestra directors.

*www.sbomagazine.com*
50 Brook Road, Needham, MA 02494
Tel: 800-964-5150
Fax: 781-453-9389

## Spirit Song

This organization offers workshops and classes that weave community singing with the ancient sound healing practice of toning.

*www.goddesschant.com/SpiritSongSeminars.htm*

76 Carlisle Road
Bedford, MA
Tel: 781-271-0130
Contact: Jan Carol

## Suzuki Association

The Suzuki Association of the Americas (SAA) is a coalition of teachers, parents, educators, and others who are interested in making music education available to all children.

**www.suzukiassociation.org**
PO Box 17310
Boulder, CO 80308
Tel: 303-444-0948
Fax: 303-444-0984

## Texas Bandmasters Association

TBA reaches out through its membership to constantly improve the quality of music education in Texas elementary, middle, and high schools, as well as in colleges and universities; presents annual convention in July.

**www.txband.com**
14501 Blanco Rd.
San Antonio, TX 78216
Tel.: 210-492-8878
Fax: 210-492-8996

## Texas Choral Directors Association

The purpose of TCDA is to secure and to maintain statewide cooperation within the choral directing profession.

**www.ensemble.org/tcda/**
404 West 30th Street
Austin TX 78705
Tel: 512-474-2801
Fax: 512-474-7873
tcda@ensemble.org

## Texas Orchestra Directors Association

Open to orchestra directors and teachers at any level, plus college level orchestra students and retired educators, TODA holds an annual convention and works throughout the year to help orchestra programs flourish and grow.

**www.ensemble.org/assoc/toda**
3728 S Cameron
Tyler, TX 95701
512-474-2801

## The Texaco Foundation

This organization offers a variety of philanthropic programs to further the cause of music education.

**www.texaco.com/support**
arts@texaco.com

## VH-1 Save the Music

This organization aims to restore music education programs in America's public schools, AND to raise awareness of the positive impact music participation has on students.

**www.vh1.com/insidevh1/savethemus/index.html**
VH1 Save The Music
1515 Broadway, 20th Floor
New York, NY 10036
Tel: 888-841-4687

# Index

# Books and Videos
# by Julie Lyonn Lieberman

## You Are Your Instrument: The Definitive Musician's Guide To Practice and Performance

Only a handful of musicians know how to create music in a fluid, pain-free manner. *You Are Your Instrument* is a comprehensive, fully illustrated, 152-page reference book designed to teach musicians how to develop a more effective as well as enjoyable experience during practice and performance, and how to heal existing injuries.

Here's what over 35 reviewers have to say about this international best-seller: "...an exceptional title...well-written...comprehensive...a must-have...an invaluable vehicle for musicians who want to learn to use their bodies and minds more intelligently while practicing and performing...her six-level approach to memorization is worth the price of the book...it should be on the shelf of every musician who wants to play without pain." ($20.00)

## Improvising Violin

Put fire in your bow! Written for the violinist who longs to leave the confines of the written page, *Improvising Violin* is a comprehensive guide to the art of violin improvisation in jazz, blues, swing, folk, rock, and New Age. This 132-page book offers dozens of exercises, riffs, stylistic techniques, patterns, chord charts, tunes, photos, quotes and anecdotes, with a preface by Darol Anger. ($19.95)

## Planet Musician

With more than 150 world scales and modes, mental and technical exercises, *Planet Musician* offers a fresh approach to music making. This innovative publication offers exciting ways for players to enrich their own musical styles by integrating ideas, techniques, and sounds from musical traditions from around the world. Comes with a 74-minute practice CD. ($23.95)

## Rockin' Out With Blues Fiddle

The blues provides a support structure and environment for incredibly powerful improvisation, especially for violinists. After all, the violin is capable of bending, sliding, moaning, whispering, and more; the violin is the closest to the voice of any instrument. This book, with its supportive practice CD, can take you from anonymous interpretive artist to expressive soloist by helping you unlock your musical imagination, fine-tune your right- and left-hand touch, and, most importantly, create your own, unique blues sound. ($21.95)

## The Contemporary Violinist

With the support of a practice CD, you will be guided through exercises and tunes designed to help you develop a feel for playing sixteen styles, including Latin, Flamenco, Gypsy, Tango, Klezmer, Cajun, Blues, Rock, Swing, Bebop, Country, Irish, Old-Time, Bluegrass, Franco-American, and Scandinavian.

This book offers seventeen tunes; dozens of left- and right-hand exercises and techniques; extensive information on each style as well as how to improvise in each genre; instrument care; new approaches to maximizing practice time; fiddle camps; equipment tips; playing healthy; fiddle on the internet; and fiddle horror stories!

With inspiring advice from Jean-Luc Ponty, Buddy Spicher, Mary Ann Harbar, Matt Glaser, James Kelly, Martin Hayes, Bruce Molsky, Jay Ungar, Mark Wood, Betsy Hill, Joe Kennedy, Jr., John Hartford, Randy Sabien, Claude Williams, Richard Greene, Stacy Phillips, Darol Anger, Michael Doucet, Leif Alpsjö, Yale Strom, Alicia Svigals, Willie Royal, Donna Hébert, Natalie MacMaster, Papa John Creach, Anthony Barnett, and Sam Zygmuntowicz! ($23.95)

## The Instrumentalist's Guide to Fitness, Health, and Musicianship

With special guests Barry Mitterhoff (mandolin/guitar), John Blake, Jr. (violin), David Krakauer (clarinet), and Sumi Tonooka (piano), as well as physical fitness trainer Michael Schwartz, Julie Lyonn Lieberman offers an ergonomic approach to music making that boosts whole-brain thinking and improves playing. You'll learn breathing and stretching techniques, warm-ups and cool-downs, and self-massage, as well as exercises to relax and center you. You'll see and feel how tension negatively affects your playing and learn how to eliminate it. 90-minute video. ($39.95)

## The Vocalist's Guide to Fitness, Health, and Musicianship

Julie Lyonn Lieberman and three highly respected experts – Maitland Peters, Katie Agresta, and Jeannie Deva – share valuable tips and hands-on tools to successfully counteract common problems faced by vocalists. In a simple, direct way, each offers advice and practice techniques addressing such important issues as breath support and control, vocal stamina, the causes of vocal dysfunction and injury, effective warm-ups and cool-downs, and the effect of diet and the environment on the body's ability to produce sound well. A lesson in vocal anatomy is included. 90-minute video. ($39.95)

## The Violin in Motion: An Ergonomic Approach to Playing for all Levels and Styles

Take a 60-minute private lesson with Julie Lyonn Lieberman on video. Her unique approach challenges the age-old "do as I do," offering violinists and violists a physiological basis for building effortless, fluid technique based on individual body type.

Sections include: holding the bow and the violin based on ergonomics; bridging from a static relationship into one that constantly breathes; the motor cortex and its relationship to music-making; factoring in your body-type when building technique; dozens of key technical tips; and a ten-minute exercise program designed specifically for violinists and violists! 60-minute video. ($39.95)

## Techniques for the Contemporary String Player

The string community is in the midst of a stylistic metamorphosis. Scores are incorporating scales, rhythms, ornaments, and textural ideas from the music of the world. Over 18 string styles have surged in popularity, including blues, swing, rock, old time, Celtic, Cajun, Cape Breton, Flamenco, Gypsy, and Latin.

Whether you want to learn a new style, be ready for anything that comes up at a jam session, or meet the demands of new orchestral scores with ease, Julie Lyonn Lieberman will help you develop the necessary skills. She has examined the technical demands of all the alternative styles and organized the most essential right- and left-hand skills into these videos.

Designed for violinists, violists, and cellists. ($34.95 each, $60 for the set)

### Part One: The Bow Hand

Four essential bow control techniques, ten approaches to rhythmizing the bow, contemporary techniques to make each note speak, and much more!

### Part Two: The Left Hand

Ten approaches to ornamentation, stylizing vibrato, use of double-stops, working with chords, slide techniques, a contemporary approach to navigating the fingerboard, and lots more!

---

### To Order Books or Videos:

**Send a check or money order to...**
Huiksi Music, P.O. Box 495, New York, NY 10024
**or call**
1-800-484-1333 and key in access code 8400

Add $5.00 shipping + $3 each additional item in U.S.A.
$8.00 + $3 each additional item, Canada;
$12.00 + $3 each additional item, Europe

**See JulieLyonn.com or write/call for a catalog.**

— DISTRIBUTED BY HAL LEONARD and IPG —

# Clinics and Residencies
# with Julie Lyonn Lieberman

Julie Lyonn Lieberman brings over 25 years of expertise as an educator and performer to her private and group teaching. A dynamic, participatory workshop leader, her ability to stimulate participants to think and grow in new ways has earned respect for her work throughout the world.

## Ms. Lieberman has presented for organizations, such as:

MENC: the National Association for Music Education; IAJE: the International Association of Jazz Educators; TODA: Texas Orchestra Director's Association; Suzuki Association; NOW: National Organization for Women; ASTA: American String Teacher's Association; and National Young Audiences.

## Her clinics and residencies have taken place in such institutions as:

Juilliard College of Music; Eastman Conservatory; Manhattan School of Music; the National String Workshop; the International String Workshop; The Mark O'Connor Fiddle Camp; New York University; New York Open Center; University of Stanford Jazz Workshop; The New School Jazz Program; Berklee College of Music; The Royal Academy of Music in Toronto, Canada; Centre for Human Performance & Health; Madeline Island Chamber Music Camp, Unison Learning Center; Cedar Rapids Symphony Orchestra; William Paterson College Jazz Department; New England Conservatory; University of Montevallo; Con Edison (upper management); and McGill University, as well as high schools and middle schools throughout the country.

### For more information on the following clinics, go to JulieLyonn.com on the web:

**The Creative Band and Orchestra**
**Playing Healthy**
**The Planet Musician Workshop**
**Improvisation**

# Soundstory and Performance Residencies
## with Julie Lyonn Lieberman

Julie Lyonn Lieberman can be booked in a one-day, three-day or five-day package to help your group develop the performance of an original soundstory created by either your ensemble or by her.

### A pre-supplied package: The Hobo Violin or The Roaring Brook Fiddler

A Lieberman soundstory consists of charts, a written story, and a brief, step-by-step training manual to help you get started. If Ms. Lieberman has to modify a pre-existing package to your needs, she requires a three-month lead-time to supply the charts. After you've had a chance to teach the charts to your students, she helps them during her residency to develop the improvised elements during the days leading up to the performance. The score and story can be modified appropriate to the playing level and ethnic backgrounds of your students or players. The residency culminates in a live performance that can include her as a narrator and/or soloist.

### An Original Soundstory

Ms. Lieberman can also come to your institution to help your players develop their own, original soundstory by teaching them how to develop compositions and a storyline, as well as helping them develop their improvisatory skills. The residency culminates in a live performance that can include her as a narrator and/or soloist.

### Performance Residency

Ms. Lieberman can present a 90-minute program, titled *The Talking Violin*, which covers styles from around the world and illustrates the five approaches to improvisation covered in this book. She can precede or follow this presentation with a training workshop for your ensemble in genre-specific improvisation.

**If you are interested in sponsoring a clinic or residency, you can contact Ms. Lieberman via Email at: Julie@JulieLyonn.com or by calling 212-724-3256**

**Julie Lyonn Lieberman**
**c/o Huiksi Music**
**P.O. Box 495**
**New York, NY 10024**

One of twelve music murals created by children at C.E.S. 11, Bronx, NY, under the direction of artist Rachel Farmer. All twelve murals are on display in the school's auditorium. Illustrations developed for this book served as the inspiration for these painted murals.